The Romance of Redemption

Studies In The Book Of Ruth

EDWARD BOONE

MBASSADOR

THE ROMANCE OF RUTH

ISBN   0 907927   87   4

First published 1936

Printed and Published by
AMBASSADOR PRODUCTIONS LTD
Providence House
16 Hillview Avenue,
Belfast, BT5 6JR. UK

*Proceeds from the sale of this book are contributed to the
welfare of Romanian orphans*

INTRODUCTION

The Book of Ruth is a gem in the treasury of the Word of God, and is of far greater importance than most readers apprehend.

Set against a dark background during a period in the history of Israel, when every man was a law unto himself, and it looked as if God's design for the nation had crashed to the ground, God's purpose is revealed.

This is the story of God's wonderful grace and great redemption. The attention of the reader will be gripped from the first page to the last.

STANLEY BARNES
HILLSBOROUGH
CO. DOWN

April, 1993

FOREWORD

I am earnestly requesting the reader to study this book with his Bible open. If he will look up the verse quoted, he will have a better understanding of God's Word, God's Plan and God's Son.

I am sending this book forth on the wings of prayer, trusting that it will be a blessing and a help to those who desire to study the Book of Ruth, verse by verse. We trust that the reader will receive as much good in reading 'The Romance of Redemption' as I have obtained in preparing it. May the blessing of the Lord, that maketh rich and addeth no sorrow, rest upon the efforts put forth, is my prayer.

I feel grateful to the Holy Spirit Who has revealed much truth to me in the months of study on the book. Throughout the study I have diligently and prayerfully sought to honour the Lord Jesus Christ, Who is so wonderfully pictured in the character 'Boaz' - the 'redeemer'. Besides this truth, much practical help may be found for the child of God who desires to be a 'gleaner' in His Word. There is also a warning note to the backslider, who has wandered away from his Father's house, with the encouragement that there is a way home.

EDWARD BOONE
Grand Rapids, Michigan

TABLE OF CONTENTS

THE STRUCTURE OF THE BOOK

There are two main divisions in the Book of Ruth, namely:

1. **"Find Grace."**   Chapters I and II.
2. **"Find Rest."**   Chapters III and IV.

It is the plan of God that the Gentiles (as Ruth) should **"Find Grace,"** "His unmerited favor," for this is the need of mankind.   Ruth said to Naomi, "Let me now go to the field, and glean ears of corn after him in whose sight I shall **Find Grace.**"   (Ch. 2:2). God's grace is so wonderful, His love so admirable, His mercy so enduring, and His fellowship so sweet that the Christian is made to ask with Ruth, *"Why have I found grace in thine eyes?"* (Ch. 2:10).

It is also the plan of God that the Gentiles should **"Find Rest."**   Naomi was so interested in Ruth that she wanted her to **"Find Rest."** (Ch. 1:9 and Ch. 3:1). The only place in the world for man to find rest is, as Ruth, at the feet of Boaz, who is a sevenfold type of Christ, as will be seen later in our study of the Book. God desires that all men should find His grace and should be delivered from the bondage of a sinful life, and then He plans for them the soul rest so clearly typified by Canaan's rest.   Thus, we see that the two main divisions of the Book show what God has planned for the Church, which is composed mostly of Gentiles.

I have divided the book into seven studies which cover, verse by verse, the entire four chapters. These we have arranged with alliterated headings.

THE TITLE OF THE BOOK

The title of the book is **"Ruth's Romance of Redemption."** The main teaching of the Book of Ruth is that there is **redemption** by the kinsman redeemer for Ruth, the Moabitish Gentile. The Gentiles are here introduced, in type, to the gospel of Christ. The burden of Paul's message contained this truth—*"That the Gentiles should be fellow-heirs, and of the same body, and partakers of his promise in Christ by the gospel."* (Eph. 3:6). The reader can readily understand how the plan of redemption for the Gentiles is taught in the book by the seven following words, which may be applied, respectively, to each of the seven studies in the book.

What a contrast there is between degradation and glorification, between the miseries of Moab and the marriage of Boaz, but here is a picture of what God does for those who are willing to follow in the footsteps which lead into the pathway of redemption.

SCOPE, SUBJECT, AND SPIRITUAL SUBSTANCE

The Book of Ruth is the history of a Jewish family, who, like the prodigal of Luke fifteen, went into the far country of Moab and there *"began to be in want."* Through the backsliding of a Jew (typified by Naomi) the poor Gentile (Ruth) is brought into the land of blessing. There Ruth meets the rich Jew Boaz and later becomes his bride. Paul brings out this truth in Romans 11:11 where he writes, *"I say then, Have they (the Jews) stumbled that they should fall? God forbid: but rather through their fall salvation is come unto the Gentiles."* In the same way, we Gentiles, (who are saved) have met the Lord Jesus Christ, as Ruth met Boaz, and some day we shall be united in marriage to Him, the New Testament Boaz. At that time the blessings will return to the Jews as they did to Naomi. The blessing bestowed upon Naomi by the neighbors was, *"Blessed be the Lord, which hath not left thee this day without a kinsman, that his name may be famous in Israel. And he shall be unto thee a restorer of thy life, and a nourisher of thine old age."* (Ruth 4:14-15). So when the bride is married to the heavenly Boaz, the Jews will bud, blossom, and bring forth fruit as did Aaron's rod in Numbers 17:8, which is typical of resurrection. Then the Jews will be raised out of the graveyard of nations and go forth to their own land, Palestine.

The Book of Ruth may be studied in the following threefold manner: (1) **Historically.** This includes the history of Elimelech and his family, the departure of Ruth from Moab to the country of Bethlehem, and her marriage to Boaz. (2) **Dispensationally.** This has been described in the preceding lines where it tells how the Jew was set aside temporarily that the Gentile might receive salvation. (3) **Typically.** We are not distinctly told in the New Testament that Boaz is a type of Jesus Christ, yet we see in his relationship to Ruth, the Gentile, as a kinsman and redeemer how beautifully he foreshadows the Lord. When we study the Book in this light, it becomes full of typical teaching. In one study of the book I have described Ruth as a type of the sinner in a sevenfold aspect, which is as follows:

> **As a Sinner She Frequented His House.**
> **As a Stranger She Found His Grace.**
> **As a Daughter She Felt His Love.**
> **As a Gleaner She Followed His Word.**
> **As a Worshiper She Fell at His Feet.**
> **As a Handmaiden She Fed at His Table.**
> **As a Bride She Finished His Plan.**

Those desiring to study the Book by chapters will find the following titles very helpful:

Chapter

   I. **THE AFFLICTION OF NAOMI.**
  II. **THE ACTIVITY OF RUTH.**

III. **THE ACKNOWLEDGMENT OF BOAZ.**
IV. **THE ALLIANCE OF THE BRIDEGROOM.**

Historical incidents frequently contain various forms of truth which are hidden to the average student of the Word of God because he does not dig deep enough beneath the surface to find the rich things that are buried there. This historical setting may be considered in the following sevenfold manner:

HISTORICAL, disclosing the past.
DISPENSATIONAL, describing Jew and Gentile.
TYPICAL, unfolding God's plan.
EXPERIMENTAL, dwelling in grace.
DEVOTIONAL, edifying the saints.
PRACTICAL, living for Christ.
PROPHETICAL, revealing the future.

Ruth and Esther are the only two books in the Bible named after women. It is extremely interesting to compare these two Books. We have no definite clue as to who is the human author of the Book of Ruth; some claim Samuel wrote it; this may be true. The chapters of the Book of Ruth might be named—

I. **THE POVERTY OF NAOMI.**
II. **THE PROVISION OF GRACE.**
III. **THE PROMISE OF BOAZ.**
IV. **THE PURCHASE OF RUTH.**

In the last study of this book, I have described Boaz as a type of the Lord Jesus Christ in a sevenfold aspect, which is as follows:

		Chapter
1.	THE REDEEMER KINSMAN	2:20
2.	THE RESTORER OF LIFE	4:15
3.	THE PROVIDER OF GRACE	2:10
4.	THE GIVER OF REST	3:1-2
5.	THE REWARDER OF SERVICE	2:15-16
6.	THE BUYER AT THE GATE	4:9-10
7.	THE LOVER IN MARRIAGE	4:13

THE DISTRESS AND THE REMOVAL

STUDY ONE

(Ruth 1:1-5)

The events recorded in the Book of Ruth took place *"when the judges ruled."* (v. 1). These are the first words of the Book. The Book of Judges gives us a survey of the condition of the people of Israel at the time the Book of Ruth was written. During the rule of the judges, the spiritual atmosphere was good when the people obeyed the Lord. The declination, however, was very apparent during these 450 years and especially toward the close of this period. The three outstanding conditions of the children of Israel as described in the Book of Judges are as follows:

1. **Disobedience**. When the Israelites would disobey the Lord, He in turn would send them chastisement from the hands of a foreign nation. When Israel would humble themselves and implore God for mercy, He would send them a deliverer—a Gideon, a Deborah, or someone to help them out of their distress. However, every time they disobeyed God, the chastisement seemed to become greater, and a longer time elapsed before they called on God for deliverance. This shows that a person's heart will become harder by continuing in disobedience.

2. **Defeat**. When the Israelites disobeyed God, He sent some nation—the Moabites, the Philistines, the Ammonites, or other enemies—who would defeat them. They destroyed their property, their crops, and

their cities. In turn, Israel would humble themselves, repent of their disobedience, and ask God for victory over their enemies. The disobedient will meet defeat. This was proved in the character of King Saul, who disobeyed the commands of Samuel and finally went down in defeat to a suicide's grave.

3. **Disgrace.** The Book of Judges describes the low and degrading moral condition of the children of Israel at that time. The 19th chapter is sufficient proof of their low standard of living. Along with the downfall of standards usually comes strife and jealousy. At this time, it existed in such a degree that brother fought against brother, and tribe against tribe. The tribe of Benjamin was so nearly wiped out at one time in cold bloody slaughter that only 600 men survived.

The Book of Judges closes with the words *"In those days there was no king in Israel: every man did that which was right in his own eyes."* (Judges 21:25). This described the condition of Israel. Each man was a law unto himself and declared, *"We are independent, we will be our own bosses."* When the laws of God, of a nation, or of a family are set aside, nothing but confusion, strife, and disorder can remain. There must be law and order to preserve peace, but here there was none, for there was *"no king in Israel."* This should be a lesson to those in the ranks of the church who would be a law unto themselves and who, regardless of the opinions of others, desire to run the church according to their own plans. Many a spiritual church has been wrecked because of church bosses that existed within their ranks. Some consider the preacher only a figurehead and not one who is called by God to lead and guide the flock. Eternity alone will reveal the grief and sorrow some ministers have had to endure because of those who wanted to be dictators on the official board or within the society of the church. Notice how different the last verse of the Book of Judges: *"And Obed begat Jesse, and Jesse begat David."* David means the *"beloved one,"* and the *"Beloved One"*—Jesus Christ—was a descendant of David.

THE NUMBER EIGHT

The Book of Ruth surely has its proper setting between the Book of Judges and the Books of Samuel. It is the eighth Book in the Bible. The number eight signifies *"a new beginning."* It is associated with resurrection—the beginning of a new order of things —for Christ arose on the first day of the week, the eighth day. *"Noah, the eighth person, a preacher of righteousness,"* (II Pet. 2:5), stepped from the ark into a new world with a total of eight people to begin, as it were, a new race. (I Pet. 3:20). The Jewish boy was circumcised on the eighth day, a type of new life, the new birth, and the new creation. The cleansed leper was presented by the priest before the Lord on the eighth day; this marked his new beginning. (Lev. 16:10-11). The eighth note in the musical scale is the note of new beginning, just as Sunday is the eighth day, the beginning of a new week. So we see from this that the Book of Ruth appropriately goes before the Books of Samuel because in the closing verse it introduces David, the eighth son of Jesse, from whom there would begin a new plan on the basis of Divine grace. The Book of Ruth describes this marvelous working of grace to the Gentile race through Jesus Christ of the seed of David. It is a bright picture on the dark background of Israel's apostasy. Just as the seventh Book of the Bible, Judges, is the number of completion, so Israel's apostasy had come to its fullness, and now God was to have a new beginning. After the rule of judges had failed, God began the order of prophets, as seen in the Book of Samuel, which follows Ruth. Just so, hundreds of years later, after the law had failed to give a man what his soul was in need of, God began His dispensation of grace through Jesus Christ, Who was of the seed of David. In this study we find the following:

> I.   THE FAMILY.
> II. THE FAMINE.
> III. THE FAILURE.

I. THE FAMILY.

There were six members in the family: Elimelech and Naomi, the husband and wife; Mahlon and Chilion, the two sons; and Orpah and Ruth, the two daughters-in-law.

THE NUMBER SIX

The number six falls short of the number of perfection, seven, thus indicating incompleteness and symbolizing fallen man without Christ. He lacks the One Who is altogether necessary to bring him into the perfect state. Man was created on the sixth day, one short of seven, which is typical of rest. The descendants of Cain are mentioned only to the sixth generation. There were six cities of refuge, provided for safety from the avenger of blood. The only safe and perfect security is in the seventh—Jesus Christ. At the marriage at Cana (John 2:6), there were six water pots of stone; these were empty and needed filling. Jesus Christ, the seventh, supplied their needs. He is the only One Who is able to bring man the blessings of which he stands in need. When Jesus was crucified, darkness began at the sixth hour. (Matt. 27:45). So, the doom of man in his eternal state without the redeeming power of Jesus Christ in his life is outer darkness. The rebellious man who rejects God will finally end with the Antichrist, whose number is 666. Goliath, the giant of Gath, who is a type of the Antichrist, was 6 cubits tall, wore 6 pieces of armor, and carried an iron spear-head weighing 600 shekels. The image erected by Nebuchadnezzar in the plain of Dura in the province of Babylon was 60 cubits high and 6 cubits wide; this is prophetic of the image that shall be erected by the Antichrist before which the world must bow in worship.

However, there is yet another character found in the Book, the seventh; his name is Boaz. He is the one who so nicely portrays the Lord Jesus Christ as the kinsman redeemer for the Gentile race. There are other characters in the Book such as the neighbors, (ch. 4:17), handmaidens, young men, the servant, (ch. 2:5), and the disabled kinsman, (ch. 4:6), but their names are not mentioned.

THE NUMBER SEVEN

The number seven represents dispensational completeness. In some places it refers to Divine fulness,

and in other places it speaks of dispensational perfection. It is composed of the numbers three and
four, the Divine and the creature in unison. Sometimes it refers to the perfection of evil as in Matthew
12:45 where seven spirits re-entered the man, and his
last state was worse than his first. God created the
world in six days but rested on the seventh in answer
to the complete satisfaction of His work. Moses was
the seventh from Abraham and to him was given the
complete law of God for the old dispensation. Enoch,
who was not, for God translated him, was the seventh
from Adam. He is a type of the church of Jesus Christ
in its dispensational completeness when it will be
raptured away to meet the Lord. There are seven
epistles, bearing the complete instructions necessary
for eternal life and godliness, written to the churches. There are seven letters written to the seven
churches in Revelation, chapters two and three, giving the complete church history from the Day of
Pentecost until its close. When the people of God
conquered Jericho, they marched around the walls
seven times on the seventh day, following seven
priests, who were carrying seven trumpets. This
displayed the perfect, complete victory of faith over
the city that was cursed. The complete and perfect
measure of forgiveness is seventy times seven as
taught by Jesus in Matthew 18:22. The seven devils
cast out of Mary Magdalene by Jesus shows the complete climax of iniquity in her life. So we see that
Boaz, being the seventh, is the one to bring about
spiritual perfection in the life of Ruth, who prefigured the Gentile church.

We are now going to study the names of each of

the seven characters, give their meaning, and then
see how nicely they fit into the picture of the Book.

A. ELIMELECH. His name means *"God is my
king."* In the days when there was no king in Israel,
there was one man, at least, who looked to the God
of Heaven to be king of his life. This shows that in
every apostasy God has a few who have stood true to
their faith in Him, just as Enoch in the antediluvian
age and Elijah during the apostasy of Ahab.

B. NAOMI. Her name means *"my pleasant one."*
Truly this is a wonderful name to have. However,
because of her life of wandering and backsliding, she
renounced the name and requested that she be called
"Mara," meaning *"bitter."* (ch. 1:20, margin). Ten
years in the land of Moab brought her home in a bitter condition.

C. MAHLON. This means *"sickly."* The offspring of Elimelech and Naomi were sickly. By in-
ference, we note the spiritual decline of the parents,
which is manifested in the names of their children.
Usually children reap a portion of what is sown by
the father and mother. When there is a decline in
spirituality at the head of the home, the effect is soon
noticeable in the children. Likewise, when the pastor
and official board of a church cease to be spiritual,
the result may soon be discerned. In the same way,
when the head officers and officials of a church or-
ganization no longer have the missionary and evangelistic spirit, and worldliness creeps into their lives,
it is soon apparent in the other avenues of the church.

D. CHILION. His name means *"consumptive."*

He is possessed with a germ and a disease that will terminate in death. Again the same spiritual drifting of the parents is being manifested in the second child but in a worse form, showing their spiritual state is rapidly declining as years go on. Throughout the Old Testament the names of the people picture the circumstances surrounding their birth. When the angel announced to Abraham and Sarah that Isaac was to be born, she laughed. When he was born, they named him Isaac, meaning *"laughter."* When Joseph was sold by his brethren into Egypt, he went through many hardships and prison experience, which finally led him to the throne. While there he married a Gentile wife, who gave birth to a son. Joseph called his name "Manasseh," which means *"He hath made me forget all my toil, and all my father's house."* (Gen. 41:51). Likewise, around these parents' lives there, no doubt, existed an unrevealed reason for them to name these sons *"sickly"* and *"consumptive."*

E. ORPAH. This means *"a portion of the neck and back."* When Naomi left Moab for the land of Bethlehem, she tried to induce her daughters-in-law, Orpah and Ruth, to return to the land of Moab, but they both declared, *"We will return with thee unto thy people."* (chap. 1:10). Again she tried to persuade them to return to Moab. *"Orpah kissed her mother-in-law; but Ruth clave unto her."* (v. 14). Thus, we see, the meaning of her name was fulfilled in her act when she turned her back on Bethlehem to worship idols in the land of Moab. How many have started like Orpah, but because of persecution, the separation the Christian life demands, or the mocking of

some friends, they turned their backs on Bethlehem-
judah to return to their idol worship again.

F. RUTH. Her name means *"satisfied."* She did
not find her satisfaction in Moab, in Naomi, or in
Bethlehem-judah, but she found it in Boaz, whom she
later married. Ruth was much like the man in the
91st Psalm, who had set his love upon the Lord, (v.
14), and because of that fact God said, *"With long
life will I satisfy him, and shew him my salvation."*
(v. 16). Many have tried to find satisfaction in different things, but the only lasting satisfaction that is
worth while for time and eternity is to be found in
Jesus Christ. Yet this satisfaction is not complete,
for man still dwells in the realms of sin, still has a
decaying body, and still lives in the midst of tempta-
tions. David sensed that fact and said, *"I shall be
satisfied, when I wake with thy likeness."* (Psalm
17:15). How we should thank God for the prospects
ahead; "It doth not yet appear what we shall be: but
we know that, when he shall appear, we shall be like
him." (I John 3:2).

G. BOAZ. His name means *"in him is strength."*
When Solomon was building the temple, he brought
out from Tyre, Hiram, who made and erected two
pillars of brass. (I Kings 7:13-22). The right pillar
he named Jachin, which means *"he shall establish."*
The left pillar was called Boaz, meaning *"in it is
strength."* Throughout the Scripture brass is typical
of judgment. The altar in the tabernacle was made
of brass, signifying that the judgment of sin was met
in the sacrifice there consumed. In the vision John
the Revelator had on the Isle of Patmos he saw Je-

sus; *"His hairs were white like wool...; his eyes were as a flame of fire; and his feet like unto fine brass, as if they burned in a furnace."* (Rev. 1:14, 15). Here Christ is not seen dressed in His high priestly garments, for His work as High Priest is completed; He now comes with His feet like unto fine brass to trample under His feet in judgment all those who have rejected the atonement He had offered. So these pillars portray Jesus Christ Who, like the sacrifice on the altar, endured the judgment for lost men. Although Solomon was a great man and able to build, in his day, a magnificent temple, there is One Who is greater than Solomon, Who shall be able to build a greater Temple, the Church of the living God. By the *strength* of His death and resurrection, He shall be able to *establish* a church against which the gates of hell will not be able to prevail. This church, composed mostly of Gentile believers, will be called *"the body of Christ."* From this we see the name Boaz points forward to Him Who is to be the descendant of David.

THE NUMBER TWO

You may wonder why there were two pillars. Two in Scripture is the number of **testimony**. Jesus said, *"In the mouth of two or three witnesses every word may be established."* (Matt. 18:16). Jesus, in answer to the challenge of the Pharisees, said, *"It is also written in your law, that the* **testimony** *of two men is true. I am one that bear witness of myself, and the Father that sent me beareth witness of me."* (John 8:17, 18). This shows us that Jesus, in defense of His Divinity, held to the law as written in Deuteronomy 17:6. As Christ is the second person of the Godhead, so He is the **testimony** of the Father for He is called in Revelation *the faithful and true witness."* The ten commandments were written on two tables of stone and were called the tables of **testimony.** (Ex. 31:18). These ten commandments express God's demand of righteousness for man. On the great Day of Atonement two scape goats were brought to the high priest, who selected one as the sacrifice upon which the sins of Israel were confessed. After the blood had been sprinkled and the sacrifice had been completed, the high priest laid his hands on the head of the live goat which was then led out to an unknown, unpopulated region of the wilderness as a **testimony** that the sins of Israel had been removed as far as the East is from the West and were remembered no more. Jesus told the disciples, *"Ye shall receive power after that the Holy Ghost is come upon you, and ye shall be witnesses unto me."* (Acts 1:8). So our testimony today should be of such a nature that men can see the power of Jesus Christ in redemption.

We find that Boaz makes the seventh character in the book—the one in whom Ruth could find her satisfaction.

II. THE FAMINE.

The setting of the first part of the Book of Ruth is Bethlehem-judah. These two words, Bethlehem-judah, with their meanings are very significant. Bethlehem, meaning the *"house of bread,"* later becomes the birthplace of Him Who was the *"Bread of Heaven,"* Jesus Christ. Judah, the tribe of which our Savior was a descendant, means *"praise the Lord."* Experimental knowledge of Him Who was born in Bethlehem produces praises unto Him Who is the Savior of the world. So in the meaning of these two words we have food and worship — nourishment for ourselves and worship for God. However, at this time, we find in this country of Bethlehem-judah, where there was supposed to have been bread and worship, a famine. In the very place where you would look for plenty, there was want. How true in many places today; where the worshipers, like Israel in the wilderness, should be fed on the *"Bread of Heaven,"* there exists nothing but a famine. Where the preaching of science, history, and current events takes the place of the Word of God, where the attendance (I was going to say worshipers) gather for social benefits, and where there is no spiritual life—just a form of religion, the worship of God in the Spirit is practically a thing of the past.

In Palestine, the country in which was Bethlehem-judah, they did not have rivers as in Egypt upon which to rely for water for their crops. They had to depend entirely on Heaven's mercy to send them rain, and if the Heavens were shut and God failed to give them rain, nothing but shortage, suffering, and death lay before them. It is the same with us in the spiritual life. If we do not have spiritual rain coming from the open heavens, it means a famine for our souls and spiritual death in the future. It seems there never was such a need of a downpouring of a spiritual, Holy Ghost rain on the places of worship as there is today in the orthodox ranks, saying nothing about the modernistic churches. In many places

worship has become so formal that scarcely an
"*Amen*" or a response can be heard to the sacred
truth.

There are three things relative to God that I would
have you notice under the subject of famine:

A. THE VIGILANCE OF GOD.
B. THE VISITATION OF GOD.
C. THE VOICE OF GOD.

A. THE VIGILANCE OF GOD. In Leviticus 26
there are two pathways outlined: the first of obedience and bestowal, the second of disobedience and
unhappiness. In considering the first, we see the order and the outcome. Four things commanded by God
are as follows: (1) **Refraining from idolatry. (v. 1).**
No idols were to have standing room in their midst,
for idolatry was an abomination to God. (2) **Regarding the Sabbath.** "*Ye shall keep my sabbaths.*" **(v.
2).** This was a day provided for bodily rest, pointing
forward to the time when we could have soul rest in
the dispensation of grace. (3) **Revering His sanctuary.** "*Reverence my sanctuary.*" (v. 2). God demands
reverence in His house. He must be revered, for He
is high and holy. (4) **Respecting God's law. (v. 3).**
He demands that they walk in His statutes and keep
His commandments. These were God's orders to the
children of Israel. The outcome with a sixfold promise may be observed in the following verses. These
all begin with the words "*I will.*" The promise of:
(a) **A Plentiful Rainfall.** "*I will give you rain in due
season.*" (v. 4). Showers of blessings were to be their
portion if they were obedient. (b) **A Peaceful Rest.**
"*I will give peace in the land, and ye shall lie down.*"

(v. 6). Peace and rest always follow obedience. (c)
A Powerful Victory. *"I will rid evil beasts out of the
land."* (v. 6). If they obeyed, their nation would be
so strong and powerful that five would chase a hundred, and one hundred would put ten thousand to
flight. (Lev. 26:8). (d) **A Prosperous Supply.** *"I will
make you fruitful."* (v. 9). Because of their faithfulness to Him, they would have things, old and new,
coming from the hand of God. Likewise, if we are
obedient, God will supply us with old and new truths
from His Word. (e) **A Place of Worship.** *"I will set
my tabernacle among you."* (v. 11). Instead of worshiping idols, they could worship the true and living
God. A place for that has been arranged. It was a
Tabernacle where they could gather, hear His voice,
and see His presence. (f) **A Pleasant Communion**.
"I will walk among you." (v. 12). They had the
promise of walking with God as Enoch of old. Just
notice the six words embraced in these promises:
rainfall, rest, victory, supply, worship, and communion. If Israel would obey His commandments,
this was God's promise to them. But God was vigilant; He saw their disobedience and tried a chasten-
ing method to bring them to Himself.

B. THE VISITATION OF GOD. As God vis-
ited Adam in the garden so He visited Israel in Canaan, but He visited them with chastisement instead
of friendship. In Deuteronomy 11:13, 14, He states,
*"And it shall come to pass, if ye shall hearken dili-
gently unto my commandments which I command
you this day, to love the Lord your God, and to serve
him with all your heart and with all your soul, That
I will give you the rain of your land in his due sea-*

*son, the first rain and the latter rain, that thou may-
est gather in thy corn, and thy wine, and thine oil."*
Here we see that God promised them rain for the
land, both the early rain to prepare the soil and the
latter rain to mature the crops. The object was that
*"thou mayest gather in thy corn, and thy wine, and
thine oil."* The drought which brought the famine
to Bethlehem-judah was a clear indication that
Israel had disobeyed God and that the Heavens were
shut.   When there is a spiritual drought in individual lives or in church organizations, it is because men have departed from the living God; because of that the Heavens are shut, and the Holy
Ghost no longer sends the spiritual rains and showers of blessings. When the Heavens fail to give the
rain, spiritual drought exists, and there is no glory
on the individuals or in the services, it is a clear indication that God is visiting with the hand of chastisement. Of course, there are testing times for every
believer, but they will not last forever. The open
Heavens that came to Christ at the time of His baptism was a sign of thirty years of perfect obedience
to the Father, for the Divine Voice spoke, *"This is
my beloved son in whom I am well pleased."* In a
similar way, God appeared to Stephen, and he testified in the closing moments of his life, *"I see the
heavens opened, and the Son of man standing on the
right hand of God."* (Acts 7:56). Because of the
faithfulness and obedience of Stephen in his message to the Jews of his day and because of his life of
faith and holiness, God opened the dome above him
and showed him His Blessed Son, Who was waiting
to welcome him—the first martyr of the New Testa-

ment. In the same way, God today visits the obedient with an open Heaven and spiritual rain from His bountiful hand, but on the disobedient He inflicts punishment by a rod of chastisement. This came to Bethlehem-judah in the nature of a famine.

C. THE VOICE OF GOD. The voice of God was a call to repentance. In mercy He was trying by a famine chastisement, to bring Israel from their false gods, from their rebellion and disobedience back to a state of worship and fellowship with Him. Some people run from the hand of chastisement and correction, as Abraham, who left the famine of Canaan and went to Egypt, and, as Elimelech and Naomi, go to Moab for help. What God wanted was a time of heart-searching. He wanted Israel to find out why the Heavens were closed. Why are we not blessed today with rain? Why must we endure this famine? Many in the ranks of Christendom have given up the fellowship of the brethren, the worship of God, and their usefulness for service and have gone into a backslidden state rather than meet the issue of God's call to repentance. A neglected Bible and a neglected secret closet soon mean a withered soul. It is impossible for a person to keep spiritually blessed by neglecting the sacred pages of the Book and the secret place of prayer. To do so means a famine for the soul, a closed Heaven, and sooner or later, the result of the rod of chastisement will be visible. This is God's method of calling the disobedient back into relationship and fellowship where they should be.

III. THE FAILURE.

They *"went to sojourn in the country of Moab."*

They did not go to Egypt, nor to Babylon, but to Moab. Rather than humbly repent and acknowledge their backslidden condition, many, as Elimelech and Naomi, have gone to Moab. There are three countries to which people living in Canaan have journeyed, Egypt, Babylon, and Moab. Let us consider them in their order.

A. EGYPT. The first five books of the Bible are full of typical teaching. The Book of Exodus brings to us Israel's bondage in Egypt. It is typical of the sinner in the world. Moses at different times mentioned the plagues of Egypt. Some people believe that leprosy originated there because it is called the **"plague of Egypt."** This is a sad picture of sin, incurable except by intervention of the Divine hand. When Joshua led Israel into the land of Canaan, God instructed him to circumcise the uncircumcised children which had been born in the wilderness during their forty years of wandering. When this was accomplished, Joshua named the place Gilgal, meaning *this day have I rolled away the* **reproach of Egypt** *from off you."* (Joshua 5:9). Again and again Israel in their murmurings wanted to turn back to Egypt. The Book of Acts teaches that *"in their hearts they turned back again into Egypt."* (Acts 7:39). The wilderness is a type of regeneration. There the children of Israel were separated, dwelling alone, not welcomed among the nations. Their guide was the pillar of cloud (typical of the Holy Spirit) which led them on their way. They were fed by heavenly manna falling daily from the skies. They drank of the water flowing from the smitten rock, which again is typical of the Holy Spirit. Egypt was **behind** them, Canaan was **before** them and God was **with** them. In the same way, the believer is delivered from this present evil world because of the blood on the door-post and the three-days' journey crossing the Red Sea, which speaks of resurrection.

Israel in Canaan is typical of the believer in a fully consecrated, sanctified state. When they reached there, they were ready for conflict. God said, *"Every place that the sole of your foot shall tread upon, that have I given unto you."* (Joshua 1:3). Here is the fight of faith, the onward march of the matured Christians led by their captain, Joshua, which means Jesus. They go from victory to victory, from glory to glory. The Christian is now dwelling in the heights of Canaan or in Heavenly places in Christ Jesus. He is resting from his own works and has the Holy Spirit's rest as is promised. He stands, like a warrior ready for battle, clothed in the armor of God, but having nothing on his back to protect him in case he should flee from the enemy. However, he has a breastplate of righteousness to face the foe. His food is no longer manna, but milk and honey, grapes and pomegranates. He is a victor, a conqueror, and an overcomer. Such is the experience of full salvation for all those who would enter into Canaan.

B. BABYLON. Babylon is the home of the back-slider and the apostate. It was there that Israel was carried after years of disobedience and rejection. They sat down on the banks of the Euphrates river and wept as they remembered Zion. While their harps hung on willows, they were requested to sing one of the songs of Zion to which they replied, *"How shall we sing the Lord's song in a strange land?"* (Psalm 137:4). This is a picture of the backslider. He is left without a song, without joy, without any bliss; he is in a state of weeping and wanting as he remembers the days of old. Babylon, according to the prophecy of Revelation 14:8, will end in utter destruction. Spiritual Babylon with its earthly corruptness is beyond healing and some day shall be destroyed. (Rev. 18:21). For that reason God calls to His own and says, *"Come out of her, my people."* (Rev. 18:4). Babylon originated with a spirit of defiance and independence toward God and took on the name of Babel. (Gen. 11:1-9). As it began so will it end, in great confusion with God's judgments resting upon it. I urge the inhabitants still in the realms of hope to heed the commands of the Word and come out of her, *"my people,"* and turn to the ways of spirituality and truth.

C. MOAB. If Egypt is typical of the world, and Babylon is the home of the backslider and apostate, what can Moab be? Let us turn to Jeremiah 48:11. There you will find the following verse: *"Moab hath been at ease from his youth, and he hath settled on his lees, and hath not been emptied from vessel to vessel, neither hath he gone into captivity: therefore his taste remained in him, and his scent is not changed."* Here we find six statements concerning those in Moab.

1. **He is Unconcerned.** *"Moab hath been at ease from his youth."* The Scripture says, *"Woe to them that are at ease in Zion."* How many we find today in

the ranks of the cold, formal church, of which Moab is typical, having no concern whatever for lost immortal souls. There is no concern for a lost world going at a rapid rate to an endless eternity; there is no soul burden or travail for those in the regions of darkness. They are at ease, having no missionary or evangelistic spirit but are self-satisfied needing nothing as the Laodicean church of Revelation, chapter three. Unless we constantly keep in a good spiritual condition, we will drift there unconsciously.

2. **He is Unfaithful.** *"He hath settled on his lees."* "This metaphor is taken from the mode of preserving wines," says Adam Clarke. "They let them rest upon their lees (dregs) for a considerable time, as this improves them both in strength and flavour; and when this is sufficiently done, they rack, or pour them off into other vessels." These are they who have settled down—doing nothing for God. Zephaniah in his prophecy states that punishment is due them: *"And I will punish the men that are settled on their lees."* (Zeph. 1:12).

3. **He is Unengaged.** *"And hath not been emptied from vessel to vessel."* The meaning of this is religious stagnation or spiritual inactivity. When a druggist fills a prescription, he takes various bottles and pours the contents into one vial. He then labels it, giving the directions on the bottle, *"Shake well before using."* He does this because if the bottle stands undisturbed for any length of time, some of the important ingredients would settle to the bottom. Thus, the medicinal virtue of the mixture would be lost. So it is with many a Christian who should be emptied

from vessel to vessel, for as God pours in, they should pour out. This truth is plainly taught in the case of Elisha and the widow. She was commanded to borrow vessels, not a few, and as long as she kept pouring, the supply of oil multiplied, which enabled her to pay the debt she owed. (II Kings 4:1). Many professors of religion, like these religionists at Moab, live only for themselves. Sacrifice is unknown to them; fasting and prayer are out of the question. They are much like the Dead Sea, always receiving but never giving. Hudson Taylor was asked, "Why is it that you are always so fresh in what you say?" "I do not know," he replied, "unless it's because I pass on in the evening what the Lord gives to me in the morning." How many there are in the formal state who are inactive. They do very little calling on the sick or personal work among the unconverted. The praying and instructions at the altar of prayer are left to someone else. Remember as you empty the vessel, He is able to refill it, providing you empty it to the benefit of someone else.

4. **He is Unpunished.** *"Neither hath he gone into captivity."* His slothful and formal condition has not yet, like Israel when she was carried into captivity, ended in judgment. This chapter closes with *"the captivity of Moab in the latter days, saith the Lord."* (v. 47). At the close of this dispensation, the saints of God who have not been at ease, who have not settled down in self-security, but who have been willing to be emptied from vessel to vessel will sit down with Jesus at the Marriage of the Lamb, during which time the Laodicean church will be called into a tremendous judgment, the seven years of tribula-

tion, which shall then fall on the earth. During these seven years of tribulation, this formal Laodicean people will fall into captivity—into the hands of the Antichrist and his God-rejecting confederates.

5. **He is Unchanged.** *"Therefore his taste remained in him."* He still has the same old appetites. If you desire the dance halls, beer gardens, card parties, movies, tobacco, and other things of the world, your taste has not been changed. A newborn soul has an appetite for the Word of God, the prayer meetings, Bible studies, secret communion, and the fellowship of the saints. He can truthfully say, "The things I once loved, I now hate." As a new creature in Christ Jesus, old things have passed away and all things have become new. A radical, instantaneous, visible transformation has occurred in his life, and he can sing with the poet, "Everything is changed; Praise the Lord."

6. **He is Undiscernible.** *"And his scent is not changed."* Scent in Scripture implies discernment. The formal, dead, professing Laodicean church and its members are without discernment. As they have no power to try the spirits to see if they are of God, they soon become an easy prey to any false doctrine that may be brought into the community or that may spring up in the Church of God. They have no ability to discern whether things are done in or out of the Spirit, nor can they detect the hypocrisy existing under the cloak of some professors. David in describing the heathen says, *"Noses have they, but they smell not."* (Psalm 115:6). This means that they have no discernment. Moses in his blessing to

the twelve tribes says of Levi, *"They shall teach Jacob thy judgments, and Israel thy law: they shall put incense at thy nose."* (Deut. 33:10, margin). The meaning of this is that the Levites, the priestly tribe, which is typical of the true Church of Christ, will be able to smell (discern) the sweet fragrance of worship that goes up from the congregation. A Levite with a flat nose was disqualified to act as priest, for he would be unable to discern whether things were good or bad. (Lev. 21:18). A man filled with the spirit of God can usually smell a spiritual camp-meeting, a prophetic Bible conference, or a Holy Ghost revival though it is many miles away. In the Song of Solomon we have the picture of Christ and the bride. In describing the bride in chapter 7:4, Solomon says, *"Thy nose is as the tower of Lebanon which looketh toward Damascus."* The bride's nose is likened to a watchtower in which the guards would sit and look toward Damascus, the city in which dwelled Israel's enemy, the Assyrians. It speaks of vigilance. In the same way, the Christian should be ever on the watch for those spiritual enemies that would invade the land of his possession, destroy his heritage, and bring him into soul bondage. However, these dwellers in Moab were not vigilant, for their scent (discernment) was not changed. This verse gives us the character and condition of the dwellers in Moab—unconcerned, unfaithful, unengaged, unpunished, unchanged, undiscernible — a type of the dead, formal Laodicean church. A six-fold description is given; this is one short of seven, the perfect number. Six is the number of fallen man without Christ.

Elimelech and Naomi left Bethlehem—the house of bread—just to sojourn in the land of Moab. Next we see they continued there. The last clause of the fourth verse reads *"and they dwelled there about ten years."* They didn't intend to stay there. They were like many folks who depart from God to seek an easier way but finally unite with the cold, dead dwellers of Moab. Some of them leave a spiritual church because they don't like the preacher, because they were unsuccessful in retaining their position on the official board, because their Sunday School class, which they had taught for a few years, was given to another, or perhaps because of even smaller things. The demotion was too great; and consequently they united with some church less spiritual.

But there's a second step downward, which I want you to notice; *"they took them wives of the women of Moab."* (v. 4). The very people whom God forbade to enter the congregation of the Lord even to the tenth generation, (Deut. 23:3), were taken as wives for the two sons, Mahlon and Chilion. Instead of remaining as a separate people, they married the very people who had previously cursed Israel under the kingship of Balak. (Num. 22). Here's a warning to parents: when you drift from the Lord Jesus Christ and from a spiritual place of worship, there is no telling what the outcome will be to you or your offspring. Unholy alliances have been the downfall of many of God's people. When Solomon took to himself wives of the Moabites, the Ammonites, and the Hittites, he began his departure from the living God. (I Kings 11:1). People often become so entangled by the meshes of the world in a backslidden state that it is very difficult and sometimes even impossible to bring them to the place where they once were. This is a warning for the young people to be sure that they make their choice in marriage according to the will of God. Many young people that were once Spirit-filled workers in God's vineyard, soul-winners in His Kingdom, have married the wrong person only to settle down to live a wasted life ending in disaster. The only life they have to live ends with want and woe.

But let us notice the outcome. Some few years after dwelling with the Moabites, separation enters the home. The rod of chastisement failed to bring Elimelech and Naomi to repentance, and now the rod of death takes the husband from the family circle of six.

A monument is erected with the name, *"Elimelech,"* inscribed upon it. He who might have had his burial in the Cave of Machpelah with Abraham, Isaac, and Jacob, now is buried, perhaps with an idolatrous ceremony, in a strange land. A few months roll by, and Mahlon is taken sick. Ere long he goes the way of all the earth; Naomi's grief increases, and Orpah is left a widow. A second tombstone is erected, and there's a second testimony that departure from God ends in disaster. The last hope that the seed-line would not be destroyed remained in Chilion, but one day they notice that his face seemed flushed; soon a red blush appears upon his cheek and a lingering disease sets in (for Chilion means consumptive). In spite of protests, tears, and sorrow, they bid good-bye to the last male who came out of Bethlehem. A third marker is erected to tell the story of the departure from God to the land of Moab.

From Bethlehem's bread to bitterness, widowhood, want, and woe—thus ends the first study of the Book of Ruth—like a cloud without a silver lining, like a dark night without a star. In conclusion, this should teach us that we cannot outrun death, that apostates die in Babylon, sinners die in Egypt, and backsliders die in Moab, that death will sooner or later overtake us in whatever country we reside or in whatever condition we may be. So it behooves us to remain in Bethlehem and take the chastisement God may send us. If your spiritual tide is low, repent and turn to Him, and the Heavens will again be opened, rain will descend, rivers will overflow, and your spiritual tide will come in. May the Lord grant this to all who read these pages.

THE DECISION AND THE RETURN
STUDY TWO
(Ruth 1:6-18)

In the preceding study the trend of Elimelech and Naomi was downward, and the general thought was **degradation.** In this study the main thought is **renunciation.** What a sad picture we have of Naomi! She is in a strange country, a land of an enemy, bereaved of husband and sons. But often the darkest hour precedes the dawn. Such was the case with Naomi.

1. **The Decision.** *"Then she arose . . . she went forth out of the place where she was."* (v's. 6, 7). As the prodigal son of Luke 15, she said, *"I will arise."* She remembered her father's house, and because of that she went **"out of the place."** It must be a decision great enough to cause you to leave the old crowd. It's one thing to arise, but it's another thing to leave the country of Moab. One of God's demands is separation. *"Come ye out from among them and be ye separate,"* saith the Lord. As long as Israel as a nation remained separate from the other nations, God blessed her. The church is a called-out body, for *"Simeon hath declared how God at the first did visit the Gentiles, to* **take out** *of them a people for his name."* (Acts 15: 14). It is because of this truth that twice-born men have no connection with the political or social realm and spirit of the world. They have been raised and made to sit together in Heavenly (not earthly) places. Their conversation (citizenship or commonwealth, F. E. Marsh) and affections are above.

2. **The Return.** *"Then she arose with her daugh-*

ters-in-law, that she might **return** *from the country of Moab.*" (v. 6). Here you will notice it gives the place from whence she was to **return**—Moab. In the following verse, it tells you the place to which she was to **return**—"*they went on the way to* **return** *unto the land of Judah.*" (v. 7). The journey from Moab to Bethlehem might be called the "pathway of repentance." It is heart-rending to compare their journey from Bethlehem-judah to Moab and that from Moab back to Bethlehem-judah. On her journey to Moab she had a husband and two boys, health, youth, and hope, but on her return she had only widowhood, want, and woe. Desolation, distress, and death had visited her, and with a broken heart she was returning to her native land. This shows that the way of the transgressor is hard. Let us note in this study—

I. **THE CAUSE.**

II. **THE CONFESSION**.

III. **THE CHOICE.**

I. THE CAUSE.

When a backslider returns to his Father's house, there is always a reason. In the story of the prodigal son, Luke 15, there were reasons that caused him to return to his home. (1) **A Divine awakening.** "*He came to himself.*" It was like a man awakening out of a sleep, for the Scripture classes man without God as one who is asleep: "*Awake thou that sleepest, and arise from the dead.*" (2) **A revelation of his need.** "*I perish with hunger.*" When a man is awakened to the fact that he is about to perish, a spirit of fear will possess him, and he will begin to look toward his Father's house for help.   (3) **A vision of good.** "How *many hired servants of my father's have bread enough and to spare.*" He remembered the bountiful supply and the table well spread with good things to eat.   Naomi, likewise, remembered the bountiful harvest in days of old, the feasts of the Lord that were held in the temple, and the great Day of the Atonement on which Israel's sins of the past year were canceled.   She, like the prodigal, was reflecting over the past years, and as a result we find "*she went forth out of the place.*"   That, however, was not the main cause for her return.   In the first verse of this study we will find three reasons which brought it about, (v. 6), namely:

A.   THE COMMUNICATION.
B.   THE VISITATION.
C.   THE PRESENTATION.

A.   THE COMMUNICATION.   "*She had heard in the country of Moab.*"   In the land where she was awakened, a message came to her from some source, for she heard that the Lord had visited His people in Bethlehem-judah.   This expresses her great need. She said, "I am hungry and in poverty, but God hath visited His people in giving them bread. I will arise; I will meet the issue; I will leave Moab and return to Bethlehem, the house of bread." Someone, unknown to the readers of the Scriptures, brought the message. No doubt, he received his reward for bringing the gospel of good news. God has had faithful messengers in all ages to tell men that there is bread in Bethlehem. Someone with a burden brought this truth to a triplet of widows in the country of Moab.

B. THE VISITATION. *"The Lord had visited his people."* This quotation of Scripture should lead us to the New Testament where Zacharias, filled with the Holy Spirit, prophesied saying, *"Blessed be the Lord God of Israel; for he hath visited and redeemed his people."* (Luke 1:68). Here it states that the object of the visitation was to redeem His people. The thought in God's mind from before the foundation of the world was redemption. Zacharias continues, telling Who this Visitor is: *"whereby the dayspring* ("sunrising" from the margin) *from on high hath visited us, to give light to them that sit in darkness and in the shadow of death, to guide our feet into the way of peace."* (v's. 78, 79). The Visitor takes on the name *"sunrising,"* and the world, which sat in darkness and in the shadow of death, was blessed with sunrise when Jesus Christ, the Son of Righteousness, the Bread of Life, was born in Bethlehem's manger. He can guide the feet into the way of **peace;** this corresponds to the song the angelic hosts sang that night, **"Peace** *on earth; good will to men."* Likewise, aged Simeon, after holding the Babe (Jesus) in his arms, could say, *"Now lettest thou thy servant depart in* **peace.**" *"Therefore being justified by faith, we have* **peace** *with God through our Lord Jesus Christ."* (Rom. 5:1).

C. THE PRESENTATION. *"In giving them bread."* (Ruth 1:6). Here is the thought of presentation. It says *"giving them bread"*—not selling it or allowing them to work for it. It was a free gift of God. The giving of this bread in Bethlehem-judah reminds us of the coming of the true Bread from Heaven as Christ later claimed Himself to be, *"I am that bread of life."* (John 6:48). We find bread is a figure of life. When Christ was born in Bethlehem, it was God's gift, the true Bread from Heaven, to a lost world. Some thirty years later, it was broken on the cross, and on the Day of Pentecost it was handed out through the Holy Spirit to a lost world, giving: (1) light to those who sit in darkness, (2) food to those who die from hunger, (3) freedom to those who dwell in bondage, (4) riches to those who live in poverty, (5) peace to those possessed with fear, (6) life to those who are in death, and (7) hope to those who dwell in misery. Since then true messengers have been giving the message to Moab, to Babylon, and to Egypt, telling the strangers and fatherless that there is bread in Bethlehem. The message that Naomi heard, she believed, and so immediately bade good-bye to Moab and, with Orpah and Ruth, her daughters-in-law, started on her lonely march to the country which God had visited.

II. THE CONFESSION.

With the return of every backslider, there must be confession. The prodigal son confessed to his father, *"I have sinned."* Without confession, repentance is not genuine. It is hard for the natural man to humble himself and pray the prayer of the publican, *"God be merciful to me a sinner."* The Scriptures teach that if man will confess and forsake his sin, he will find mercy. In my ministry, I find that it is much harder for backsliders to get back into relationship and fellowship with God than for an out-and-out sinner who has never been converted. The reason is the backslider has sinned against light. The greater degree of light a sinner has the harder it usually is for him to find God. This can be proved by the way the Jews and Gentiles received the Holy Ghost. The Jews, who were in the covenant and were children of promise, had to tarry ten days (some teach seven) for the outpouring of the Holy Spirit, (Acts 2), but the Gentiles, who were afar off, having little light and no hope in the world, received the Holy Ghost while Peter was yet speaking. (Acts 10). In the latter case, there was no tarrying, supplication, or waiting on God, but while Peter was bringing the message, the Holy Spirit came upon them in like manner as on the Jews at Pentecost. Thus, the Jews could not claim that they had any supernatural manifestations that the Gentiles did not have.

After Naomi, Orpah, and Ruth were some distance from Moab. Naomi tried to induce her daughters-in-law to return to their native land, (v. 8), praying that the Lord might deal kindly with them and grant them rest in the houses of their husbands. Then she kissed them, and they wept bitterly saying, *"Surely we will return with thee unto thy people."* (v. 10). Again Naomi tried to persuade them to return and then confesses—

    A. HER HOPELESSNESS.
    B. HER HELPLESSNESS.
    C. HER HAPLESSNESS.

A. HER HOPELESSNESS. She asked them the question, *"Why will ye go with me?"* (v. 11). "I am too old to have more sons. Would you want to wait that you might unite with them in marriage in order to restore the sacred seed-line and redeem back the lost property?" This was the thought that Naomi had in mind, and it grieved her to think her daughters-in-law were left in such a condition with no kinsman to redeem the estate in Bethlehem. She, a widow in want and woe, was stripped of all her possessions, going back over the lonely road to her father's house. What a picture of repentance!

B. HER HELPLESSNESS. *"It grieveth me much for your sakes."* (v. 13). She grieves much over the situation because she feels that she is responsible for the fate of the two girls. By this statement she acknowledges, "I am the sinner, but you are the sufferers. I have disobeyed God in bringing my sons to the land of Moab where they intermarried against His commandments. Because of this, the hand of the Lord is upon me; it grieves me for your sakes." This shows that no man liveth or dieth to himself. He either helps to take men to Heaven or helps to drag them down to hell. Your life either lifts your loved ones, neighbors, and friends, or causes them to drift farther from God. I was saved nineteen years ago. It was several years before any of my relatives were saved, but in the past six years I have had the privilege of seeing two sisters, two brothers, one brother-in-law, one nephew, one neice, and several other relatives brought to the Lord, most of them directly through my own ministry. Beloved, if you are living in the realm of grace, you cannot help but lead your friends to a higher life. Many children are not saved because their parents do not live close enough to God. Had Naomi stayed in the land of Bethlehem, it might have spared Orpah and Ruth many sorrows, and, likewise, if people would remain in fellowship and relationship with God, it might spare them and others of their family much distress and grief. One more thought is worthy of our comment: Naomi was ready to shoulder the blame. Many backsliders will blame some one else for their failures, but in reality no one is to blame but themselves.

C. HER HAPLESSNESS. This means unhappiness. *"That the hand of the Lord is gone out against me."* (v. 13). Did you ever see anyone prosper while the **hand of the Lord** was against him? Would you rather be in the hollow of His hand or have His hand against you? What a thought—**"the hand of the Lord!"** Let us notice *"the hand of the Lord"* in the following three cases. (1) In the case of Elijah. When he stood before Ahab and Jehoshaphat, they requested him to prophesy the outcome of the battle with the Moabites. So he called for a minstrel, and it says, as the minstrel played, "the hand of the Lord came **upon** him." Here you will notice the hand of the Lord **upon** Elijah in revelation, instructing him. God planned to give Israel victory in the battle as foretold by Elijah. (II Kings 3:14-16). (2) In the case of the disciples who were scattered as a result of the persecution of Stephen. They traveled to Phenice, Cyprus, and Antioch, preaching the Word of God, and the Scripture says, "The hand of the Lord was **with** them: and a great number believed, and turned unto the Lord." (Acts 11:21). Here you will notice the hand of the Lord **with** them in service or soul-winning. A great number believed and turned to the faith because the disciples were going forth in the strength of the Lord. In fact, that is the only way of achieving successful soul-winning. That which is done by human efforts and through human accomplishments is not a success. What we need in soul-winning as well as in every department of the work of God is the Holy Spirit in our lives. (3) In the case of Naomi when she acknowledged that the hand of the Lord was **against** her. (Ruth 1:13). Thus we see the hand of the Lord may be **upon** man, **with** man, or **against** man. It is possible for the hand that was wounded for our redemption to be against us. Naomi realized that the hand of the Lord was not only against her, but in the superlative degree was heavily against her. Markers on the graves of the husband and two boys and by the fact that there was no kinsman to carry on the seed-line or redeem the lost estate of Bethlehem-judah nor a bread-earner for her daughters-in-law or herself all showed that the hand of the Lord was heavily against her. They were strangers now to the old form of worship and were not in fellowship with God. What could she do in this dilemma? There was only one help. She must humbly seek the mercy of the Lord Jehovah, forsake the idolatrous country of Moab, make a complete separation, and go back to the place from which she came. Thus we have seen Naomi in her hopelessness, helplessness, and haplessness.

III. THE CHOICE.

Why did Naomi try to induce the two widows, Orpah and Ruth, to return to their own land? I believe the lesson we should learn from this is that every soul will be tested, to see if they will follow the Lord on the basis of pure love for Him. Those who follow the profession of Christianity only because of their relatives, because of an obligation to their friends, or for the sake of pleasing their company will be converts of small value and short duration. If Orpah and Ruth insisted on going with her to Bethlehem, Naomi would not have them go on her account but purely in love for God. She would have them make it their deliberate choice and count the cost of leaving Moab and going to Bethlehem. Oh, if men who start for Heaven would first consider the separation that God demands, the persecution which may be involved, and, in the face of that, make a final surrender, there would be more folks enduring to the end. This truth Jesus desired to present to the young man who came to Him and said, *"Lord, I will follow thee whithersoever thou goest."* Jesus, to test the validity of the young man's statement, said, *"Foxes have holes, birds of the air have nests; but the Son of man hath not where to lay his head."* (Luke 9:57, 58). In the same manner, Naomi deals with her daughters-in-law.

Orpah returned to her **relatives** and to her **religion**. *"Thy sister in law is gone back unto her people* **(relatives),** *and unto her gods* **(religion)."** (v. 15). There are certain conditions that must be met by those coming to Jesus Christ for the remission of their sins. Two of these are the giving up of **relatives** and the surrendering of **religion.** How often **relatives** have hindered people from going with God. A wife, a husband, a brother, a sister, or some other member of the family is often the influential factor in the lives making the wrong decision. Likewise, it is difficult for many to give up their **religion,** religion without salvation. Yes, many are church members and through baptism or confirmation have been so from the first few months of their lives, but they have never been born again. One of the hardest things in the world is to get a person to give up a false religion or a religion with no life or spirituality. So Orpah and Ruth were tested to see whether they were ready to give up **relatives** and **religion.** Jesus said, *"So likewise, whosoever he be of you that forsaketh not all that he hath, he cannot be my disciple."* (Luke 14:33). Besides these, there are other reasons why people do not make a complete surrender, such as social prestige, the riches of this world, the opinions of people, the separation demanded, and other things too numerous to mention.

There are six items in Ruth's decision. These will be studied in couplets. (1) *"Whither thou goest, I will go"* and *"where thou lodgest, I will lodge."* (2) *"Thy people shall be my people"* and *"thy God my God."* (3) *"Where thou diest, will I die"* and *"there will I be buried."* Her consecration could go no farther than the grave, for without Divine life one has no hope beyond that realm. Nevertheless, her consecration was complete as far as it could go, for there was no provision made for returning to Moab, and according to her statement, nothing but death could separate them. There are six items in this decision—one short of the number seven, the seventh being provided by the resurrection of Christ. The man or woman *"in Christ,"* having eternal life, can look beyond the grave and see "A land that is fairer than day; And by faith we can see it afar." Let us view these three couplets in the following order:

A. HER SUBMISSION. *"Whither thou goest, I will go"* and *"where thou lodgest, I will lodge."* Her surrender was so complete that she desired to walk in the footsteps of another. *"Whither thou goest, I will go."* (v. 16). In like manner, the natural consequence of salvation will be a desire to walk in the footsteps of Jesus and to follow where He leads us. It may seem hard at times, but it is the pathway that leads to Heaven, as seen in the life of Christ. After thirty-three years of earthly trials, hardships, misunderstandings, persecutions, and finally death, He was raised to the right hand of the Throne of God. Jesus said, *"He that taketh not his cross and followeth after me is not worthy of me."* Likewise, Ruth left the land of the curse for the land of the covenant.

"Where thou lodgest, I will lodge" is the second condition under the heading, "Submission." She has completely renounced all freedom of choice and commits herself into the care and keeping of another. Where Naomi lodged, she desired to lodge. Why? That she might have communion. Our lodgment may not be the best here on earth, but if we have Jesus, it will be a paradise. Ruth made no demands as to the place where she was to lodge. Her one and great desire was that she might be in the company of the one to whom she had committed herself. Likewise, we as Christians, regardless of the place where we must lodge, desire the companionship and presence of Jesus more than anything else. We may have, like Jacob of old, a stone for a pillow, but we are awakened to find that God is in the place. We can sing with the poet of old—

"A tent or a cottage, why should I care?
They're building a palace for me over there!"

To lodge with Him here means that we shall dwell with Him hereafter. Ruth may be classed with those in Revelation who *"follow the Lamb whithersoever he goeth."* (Rev. 14:4). Her whole future life was veiled, but her faith and confidence held fast in one whom she knew would lead the way aright. If she lodged with Naomi, the responsibility of her support and her keeping would be in the hands of the one whom she desired to follow. Likewise, the believer who yields completely to Christ may look to Him as the source of his supply.

B.   HER ACCEPTANCE. *"Thy people shall be my people"* and *"thy God my God."* (v. 16). This meant a separation from all her old associates and an **acceptance** of a people whom she had never known. For this act Boaz compliments her and says, *"It hath been fully shewed me, all that thou hast done unto thy mother-in-law since the death of thine husband: and how thou hast left thy father and thy mother, and the land of thy nativity, and art come unto a people which thou knewest not heretofore."* (Ruth 2:11). Between the people of the world and the followers of Christ, there is a line of demarcation, for God's people are not of the world though they live within its sphere. As in the case of Israel and the Egyptians (Ex. 10:13), on the one side of the line is darkness; on the other side there is light; there can be no affinity. The connecting links of the former fellowship are severed when we come to Christ. Ruth's definite decision proclaimed her severance from Moab and all its idolatrous worship.

She went a step farther and said *"thy God shall be my God."* This brings her into the realm of worship. The idols of Moab are left behind and she, like the Thessalonians, *"have turned to God from idols to serve the living and true God."* (I Thess. 1:9). She makes this a personal matter and says, "He shall be **my God.**" She wanted a personal God for propitiation, power, protection, and provision. David made a similar statement when he said, *"The Lord is* **my shepherd;** *I shall not want."* He embraces Him as his own personal shepherd. From now on, Israel's God was to be Ruth's object of worship. What a step of faith on the part of Ruth. So it is with everyone that turns to the Lord Jesus Christ and claims Him as his own personal Savior.

C. HER CONSECRATION. *"Where thou diest I will die"* and *"there will I be buried."* Her consecration went as far as the last breath of her earthly career. Whether this was a few days or of long duration, every moment, every hour, every day, every year was involved in the consecration. She was making a decision that would never be reversed or altered. It meant good-bye to Moab, home, and everything. *"No man,"* says Jesus, *"having put his hand to the plough and looking back is fit for the kingdom of God."* (Luke 9:62). From this we see Ruth was not like Lot's wife, who looked back and was turned to a pillar of salt, but she set her face steadfastly toward Bethlehem. To follow in the footsteps of Christ, to go where He goes, to lodge where He lodges, and to die where He died will lead you to Gethsemane and to Calvary. It will take you up to Golgotha's brow, and there you will see the agony Christ endured, the punishment He bore, the separation He chose, and the death He died. Moreover, you will be able to say, *"I am crucified with Christ, His death is my death,"* but you can still go further and say, *"Nevertheless, I live, and His life is my life."* You have the hope of the coming resurrection which is the unmentioned item in Ruth's choice.

The climax of the six items is *"there will I be buried."* Her love had reached its highest peak and its greatest abandonment. One has said, "The life has been surrendered in blank." She had pursued this earthly life to its farthest goal. Beyond the cemetery her consecration could not go. How unlike the natural man was she, who thinks of this life only, who lives as if it terminated in death, seldom thinking of the life beyond the grave. However, a more thorough, complete, and deeper consecration could not be made, for she did not want even her bones, the remains of her earthly career, to be buried in Moab. She desired her remains to lie on God's territory, in Canaan's possession. Likewise, Joseph requested in his departing hour that his embalmed body be taken from Egypt and buried in Canaan. (Hebrews 11:22). Hundreds of years later, Moses took the bones of Joseph with him as he crossed the Red Sea on his journey to Canaan. (Exodus 13:19). A consecration so complete and thorough that the world (Egypt) and cold formality (Moab) could have no claims on even the final remains of her earthly house is certainly worthy of comment.

THE CAVE OF MACHPELAH

A typical picture is seen in the case of Abraham purchasing a burying place for his wife, Sarah. (Gen. 23). In the preceding chapter, verses 20 to 24, Abraham had heard from his native land, Chaldea, how Milcah, the wife of Nahor, Abraham's brother, had given birth to several children. Having heard this recent message about his kindred, it was natural that he should desire to bury Sarah among his own people. Yet for certain reasons, Abraham chose to bury his dead in a strange land apart from his kindred and home circles. The thought of a future resurrection from the grave was one of the strong doctrines embraced by dear old Abraham, the man of faith. This is shown when he made preparation to offer up his son, Isaac, on Mount Moriah. He did it on the grounds *"that God was able to raise him up, even from the dead; from whence also he raised him in a figure."* (Hebrews 11:19). So in purchasing this cave as the resting place for the bodies of himself and family, his faith challenged death and said, *"we shall live again,"* looking forward to a coming resurrection. Palestine with its fertility and abundance of riches could have provided for Abraham a permanent home, a place in which he could settle and abide throughout the remainder of his earthly career. However, he chose rather to dwell in tents, as a stranger and pilgrim, having no certain dwelling place that he might look forward for the eternal inheritance that God had promised him as a reward for his step of faith and obedience. Likewise, we who renounce the spirit and life of this world declare with Abraham that we seek a city whose builder and maker is God.

But why should Abraham bury his loved ones in Canaan's land apart from his kindred and home surroundings? By this Abraham expressed his faith in God and in the coming resurrection, at which time he would be heir to the land of promise which God promised him upon leaving Chaldea. This act was equivalent to saying that he believed this country would remain perpetually the country for his children and his people. He had lived as a pilgrim and a stranger in the earth, had abandoned his fatherland, and had refrained from buying land or houses in Canaan. The first property then that Abraham had as his own posession was the grave of Machpelah. This was a testimony that he claimed the land of Canaan, which God promised him, as his future possession. It was property that he could not exchange, sell, or abandon; it was his as long as the dead remained within its possession. He refused an offer of the children of Heth to use one of their sepulchers. This had to be his own property, purchased by his own hand at the gate of the city where all business was transacted in the presence of the people of the land so that they might witness to the fact that Abraham had bought with a stipulated amount of silver the burying place which was to be his own possession as long as the sacred dust remained within its realms. This transaction had to be recorded on the records of that time so that no usurper or dishonest landgrabber could come forth and claim the possession as his own. This had to belong to Abraham without question or doubt.

Four hundred shekels of silver, current money with

the merchant, was the price of the burying ground.
(Gen. 23:16). Silver throughout the Scripture speaks
of atonement or redemption. In Exodus 30:11-16, we
find the Lord's instructions to Moses regarding the
half shekel of silver which the Israelites were to
bring to the priest, who, in turn, would scrutinize
the coin to see that it was not a counterfeit but a genuine coin according to the shekel of the sanctuary.
When this was done and the silver shekel passed
upon, his name was recorded in the records of Israel,
and he was numbered with the ransomed.   This
shekel was called the atonement money, (v. 16),
which was the ransom price for the soul. (v. 12).
This gives us the thought of redemption. In turn,
this money was all used in the construction of the
tabernacle. It went to form the foundation of the
tabernacle proper on which the boards and bars
rested. This is typical of the House of God which
stands upon the ransom price of the redemption of
Jesus Christ. No wonder the song writer said:

> "On Christ, the solid Rock, I stand;
> All other ground is sinking sand."

Peter referred to this atonement money by way of
contrast when he wrote, *"Forasmuch as ye know that
ye were not redeemed with corruptible things, as
silver and gold, from your vain conversation received
by tradition from your fathers; But with the precious
blood of Christ."* (I Pet. 1:18-19). He, no doubt, mentioned atonement money, which was, as we just
stated, the price of redemption, to show how this
atonement money pointed forward to the time when
Christ would, with His own blood, be the ransom

price for our redemption. Thirty shekels of silver
was the price for which Jesus was sold by the hand
of Judas. The word *"silver"* is used for the first time
in the Scriptures in connection with father Abraham
—the man of faith. The first time silver was used
for the purchasing of any material product or land
was in the case of Abraham buying from the children of Heth the sepulcher for Sarah, himself, and
family. This was to remind us that a life of peace
and rest beyond the grave through the hope of the
coming resurrection, when the graves shall give up
their dead, can be based only on the price of redemption.

Therefore, on the grounds of death and resurrection, Abraham, Isaac, and Jacob, (Heb. 11:9), became heirs of the Holy land in which their sacred
remains now lie, waiting for the blowing of the
trumpet when the dead in Christ shall rise to claim
their inheritance, which was promised them by the
God Who was not ashamed to be called their God.
(v. 16). People who live only for this life cannot
and do not please God. He is ashamed to be identified with them. All of man—spirit, soul, and body—
must look forward to the period beyond the resurrection. Ere long Abraham and his descendants will
enter into their inheritance of one thousand years
of peace on this earth, Palestine being the capital and
headquarters. Because of this anticipation, Abraham purchased for himself a burying place far from
his native land of Chaldea so that when his sacred
remains of dust shall rise from corruption, he would
stand on the very territory that was given him as his
inheritance. The land of Canaan was promised to

Abraham as his possession for his faith and obedience to God, but the Scriptures teach that he died in the faith, not having received the promises or the inheritance but having seen them afar off. (Heb. 11:13). There can be only one possible outcome, that is, Abraham will yet receive this inheritance that God has promised him.

This brings us back to the thought of Ruth where she says, *"Where thou diest, will I die"* and *"there will I be buried."* The seventh unmentioned item of Ruth's consecration may be embraced in these words, *"For if we be dead with him (Christ), we shall also live with him."* (II Tim. 2:11). *"Who died for us, that, whether we wake or sleep, we should live together with him."* (I Thess. 5:10). When Naomi saw that she was *"steadfastly minded to go with her,"* (Ruth 1:18), she was silent and was convinced that Ruth had made the choice, not because of human ties but on the grounds of faith that there was bread (Christ) in Bethlehem. May many others make the same clear-cut decision and, as Ruth, be satisfied and finally unite in marriage with Boaz, the Christ of Bethlehem.

THE DAMAGE AND THE RECEPTION

STUDY THREE

(Ruth 1:19-22)

The third study of the book opens with the words, *"So they two went until they came to Bethlehem."* Two, Ruth and Naomi, were returning. As two, referred to in study one, is the number of testimony, this study is a testimony of the damage and loss of ten years of wasted life in Moab. There are various places in Scripture where two walked together. **First,** in the case of the two disciples on the way to Emmaus, we find that their conversation was about the crucifixion of Christ. (Luke 24:20). In this case, we have the testimony of two men regarding the condemnation and crucifixion of our Saviour. **Second,** in the case of Elijah and Elisha. Having crossed the Jordan River after its smiting and dividing—typical of the death and the resurrection of Christ—Elijah asked Elisha what he could do for him before he was taken away. *"And Elisha said, I pray thee, let a double portion of thy spirit be upon me."* (II Kings 2:9). Here we have the testimony of two men relative to the double portion, typical of Pentecost. **Third,** in the case of Enoch and God, who had walked together in unbroken fellowship for the long period of three hundred years. (Gen. 5:22). The conversation in this case, no doubt, was the translation of Enoch, for he was *"translated that he should not see death; and was not found, because God had translated him."* (Heb. 11:5). Here we have the testimony of the rapture of the saints. Thus, in these three cases we find that the conversation was about the cruci-fixion of Christ, the descent of the Holy Spirit and the rapture of the saints. Likewise, in the returning of Naomi and Ruth to Bethlehem, we have the testi-mony that the way of the transgressor is hard, that the way of the backslider ended in widowhood, want, woe. Such is the danger taught in this lesson.

However, there is an encouraging thought to those who may be backslidden or to the man or woman out of complete victory that there is a re-ception for the wanderer who will return to the Fa-ther's house. The fifteenth chapter of Luke gives us a blessed picture of the reception of the prodigal son. The father was more willing to receive his son than his son was to be received. If the reader may have wandered from God, return at once to the Father's house. He wants you home. You will find a wel-come not only from the hand of your Heavenly Fa-ther, but His children also will welcome you to your former place of worship. The devil will try to make you think that no one loves you, that there's no use to try, but the following lines should encourage your heart:

> You may say I'm so unworthy,
> There's no use for me to try
> I have always been rebellious,
> In my sin I'll have to die,
> Though your state may be appalling,
> Hear the Saviour calling,
> Saving grace is falling,
> Just for thee.

If the father could forgive the prodigal and feed him at his table, if God could forgive David and set him on the throne, if God could forgive scores and scores of backsliders and write their names in the Book of Heaven, He can forgive you. In studying this lesson let us notice—

I. THE GREAT SURPRISE.
II. THE GRIEVOUS SORROW.
III. THE GRATIFYING SUPPLY.

I. THE GREAT SURPRISE.

The conversation that took place on their journey from Moab to Bethlehem is not recorded. Some may wonder why, but the reason is that it pictures the road of repentance, and that is a matter that lies strictly between the soul and its God. The idea of having to confess to a priest or preacher for forgiveness of sins is unscriptural, for our repentance is toward God, and our faith should be in the Lord Jesus Christ alone. This was the message that was preached by the early apostles. (Acts 20:21). There is nothing mentioned relative to the hardship of the journey, the weather conditions, or the mode of travel, which was probably by foot. But Naomi, no doubt, talked much of the country of Bethlehem just as we would in leading a sinner to Christ. In considering the return, let us note—

A. THE EFFECT. *"Is this Naomi?"* (v. 19). You will notice that she is greeted with a question. Why should they ask, "Is this Naomi?" There must have been a reason. No doubt, she bore the marks of Moab. Ten years spent in the land of death and formality had removed from her the blush of spiritual youth, the might of spiritual power, the radiance of spiritual glory, the quietness of spiritual peace, the harmony of spiritual fellowship, the covering of spiritual garments, and the blessing of spiritual joy. Have you ever seen people who once enjoyed these splendid spiritual qualifications, drift to a land of spiritual Moab and come back looking more like Broadway Avenue flappers than like a stranger and a pilgrim? They are dressed in the latest fashions, their cheeks are covered with rouge, their lips have the appearance of a setting sun on a June evening, from their ears are hung ornaments making them look much like the heathen of Moab, and I speak to their shame, some finger-tips are well tinted with brown from the constant use of cigarettes. Such has been the case of some who have left Bethlehem-judah because of chastisement and correction; the effect has been so great that many have exclaimed, "Is this Naomi? Is this the one who attended the prayer meetings, blessed the congregation with her prayers and testimonies that exalted Jesus Christ? Is this the one who loved Divine truth?" It is a picture which should make an angel weep.

Robbed of all the pleasantness that grace provided; stripped of all the glory that His Spirit brings; living in the deepest depths of worldliness and sin—such is a picture of some who have joined the ranks of the backsliders. Included in these ranks, you will find evangelists, pastors, class leaders, Sunday School superintendents, Sunday School teachers, Bible School students, and young people who were brought up in godly homes. What a dark picture! What a sad story! Nevertheless, it is true. After studying the effect, let us notice—

B.   THE SYMPATHY. *"All the city was moved."*
(v. 19).   As the two wayworn strangers marched
through the dusty roads of the city, some of the citizens are seen gazing, with a look of interest, through
their windows, from their fields, or other places of
occupation. When they finally arrived at their desti-
nation, *"All the city was moved* **about** *them."* Soon
a large company gathered around them. *"Is this
Naomi?"* one old lady asks. "Are you the one whose
wedding I attended years ago?" She replies in the
affirmative. No doubt, they ask, "Where is Elimelech?" And she tells the story of his sickness and of
his final departure. A middle-aged Israelite comes up
and questions her regarding Chilion saying, "We
were schoolmates." When Naomi is asked about the
welfare of Chilion, more tears flow down her cheeks
as she tells the story of his sickness and his last
words. Then comes the rabbi, whom she remembers
as the one who blessed the congregation of the Lord
in which her family was numbered. As he recalls
the ceremony when Mahlon was circumcised on the
eighth day, he questions Naomi, who, amidst her sobs,
relates the sad story of his lingering illness, his fare-
well gaze, his last words, and his final departure. As
she tells of her loneliness, of her visits to the graves
in the village cemetery, of the sleepless nights, the
deepest poverty, the homesickness for Bethlehem, it
arouses her old community and neighbors to
sympathy, and they weep with her who weeps as she
describes her life of sorrow, suffering, and separation.

The city is moved as the news of her loss, loneliness, and return spreads from door to door. How-

ever, Bethlehem is not the only city that has been moved by the return of the backslider, for all Heaven rejoices more when one sinner repents than over ninety-nine just persons who need no repentance. The Lord of Heaven has made it known that the whole City, whose Builder and Maker is God, is moved to shouts of joy and gladness when one sinner forsakes the life of sin and wandering and returns to the house of bread—Bethlehem. Though the citizens of earth may be little interested in a Holy Ghost revival, or in the conversion of a sinner, yet the City without foundation, eternal in the Heavens, is interested and is acquainted with the results of the efforts put forth for lost men. Sympathy! Yes, there is lots of it for the wanderer who will humbly and wholly return. First, there is sympathy from the hand of His Father; second, from the citizens of Bethlehem, who portrays the church; third, from all Heaven itself. Let us now consider—

C. THE WELCOME. As Naomi had no way of earning her livelihood, she probably would have to be a city or community charge. As far as she knew, there was no kinsman to redeem for her the lost estate, where she once resided, and to provide for her the necessities of life. Neither was there one to restore the seed-line, which was destroyed by their trip to Moab. This was a reproach in itself even to those who remained in Bethlehem-judah. What made it still harder was that she had the responsibility of the Moabitish damsel—a Gentile, forbidden to gather in the congregation of the Lord, a stranger, and an outcast who could stand only in the far-off place. Would there be a welcome for those who represent the Jew and Gentile? Yes, thank God, there is under the dispensation of Grace, which the Book of Ruth so wonderfully pictures.

The middle wall has been broken down. Paul describes this in Ephesians 2:14. Doctor Edersheim in his book "The Temple, Its Ministry and Services" writes, "The great Court of the Gentiles, which formed the lowest or outer enclosure of the Sanctuary, was paved with the finest variegated marble. According to Jewish tradition, it formed a square of 750 feet. Its name is derived from the fact that it was open to all —Jews or Gentiles." He continues, "Within a short distance, in the court, a marble screen 4½ feet high, and beautifully ornamented, bore Greek and Latin inscriptions, warning Gentiles not to proceed (beyond this wall) on pain of death." By this wall and inscription, the Gentiles were barred outside of the Holy place, but with the salvation of Jesus Christ, the middle wall was broken down, and we are made nigh by the blood of Christ. Now we are invited to come boldly to a throne of Grace by the new and living way which Christ has provided for us, that whether we be Jews or Gentiles, we will find a hearty welcome.

II. THE GRIEVOUS SORROW.

All Naomi could bring back from the land of Moab was the remembrance of her fate and folly. Those ten years—ten years of wasted life—could never be recalled or re-lived. Her sad condition is a picture of the evil and bitter result of departing from the Lord. This should be a warning to all not to turn from the

Grace of God to a life of formality, worldliness, or sinfulness. What havoc her departure had brought, and she is now forced to acknowledge the reason for her sad state. Let us notice the following three items regarding her return:

    A.   THE SPIRIT.
    B.   THE STATE.
    C.   THE SORROW.

A.   THE SPIRIT IN WHICH SHE RETURNED. *"Call me not Naomi, call me Mara."* (v. 20). You will notice she completely surrenders the name Naomi, which means *"my pleasant one,"* and is willing to take the name Mara, meaning *"the bitter one."* She feels she is no longer worthy to be called Naomi. She is like the prodigal son, who said, *"Make me one of thy hired servants."* The further we study the Book of Ruth, the more we see the parable of the prodigal son portrayed. It does not infer that she retained a bitter spirit toward the Almighty, but rather that her heart was grieved over her own condition. It is a picture of a broken and a contrite heart. There is many a child of God whose name was Naomi, but who has lost that sweet name. It is no longer "my pleasant one," but now she is called Mara, *"the bitter one."* Moab is the land of bitterness to the child of God, but Bethlehem is the land of bread. This spirit of bitterness often exists in backsliders, who return to God. Although God has forgiven them and their wanderings are all under the blood never to be remembered against them, seemingly they are unable to forgive themselves and thereby remain under a certain amount of bondage. Beloved, if that is your case to-

day, remember if God has forgiven you, your sins
will never be brought up again. Lift up your head,
go forward, for God is able to restore the years in
which the locusts have destroyed the results of your
efforts.

B. THE STATE IN WHICH SHE RETURNED.
*"I went out full, and the Lord hath brought me home
again empty."* (v. 21). Again we see a likeness in the
parable of the prodigal son, who said, *"Father, give
me the portion of goods that falleth to me."* He went
out full and, as Naomi, came back empty. Paul in
writing to the Corinthians said, *"Ye are full."* (I Cor.
4:8). That is the privilege of every believer. (1) As
Barnabas, we should be **"full of the Holy Ghost."**
(Acts 11:24). This gives us the thought of Divine
power. What a contrast between this and elocution,
oratory, psychology, emotions, and human efforts
which are being used so extensively these days in
place of the Holy Spirit to do the work of God! (2)
As Stephen, we should be **"full of faith,"** (Acts 6:5),
which speaks of steadfastness, for faith comes from
the Greek word *"pistis,"* meaning *"to be faithful or
steadfast."* A splendid qualification of a believer is
to be faithful or steadfast, always abounding in the
work of the Lord. This is the privilege of every one
providing he is filled with the Holy Spirit. A carnal
believer is never faithful or steadfast. "A double
minded (carnal and spiritual mind) man is unstable
in all his ways." (James 1:8). (3) As strangers and
pilgrims, we should be **"full of glory."** (I Pet. 1:8).
This denotes Divine presence which these persecuted
sufferers of Pontus, Galatia, and Cappadocia possessed. It is the right of every believer to have the sacred

presence of His Glory to aid him through every test and trial, but he can also have it in testimony and prayer. There is very little praying in the Holy Ghost today and little testimony and exhortation given by speakers upon whom Divine unction rests. May God keep us full of glory. (4) As Dorcas, we should be **"full of good works."** (Acts 9:36). This indicates fruitfulness. It is as natural for the new life in the believer to produce the fruits of righteousness as it is for water to flow down stream. It is not necessary to force ourselves to live righteous, we just can't help but do it. Twice-born men do not quit their swearing, their blaspheming, or their meanness because they have to, but it is removed from their lives by the power of God. Twice-born men are filled with fruitfulness today as well as on the day of Pentecost. (5) As the apostles, we should be **"full of new wine."** (Acts 2:13). This is typical of joy. When Jesus turned the water into wine, it was typical of how He would turn the lives of spiritual emptiness into lives of victory and joy. Jesus gave the lesson of the vine and the branches to show the disciples that the consecration of their lives would result in fruitfulness and in fullness of joy. *"These things have I spoken unto you, that my joy might remain in you, and that your joy might be full."* (John 15:11). *"The joy of the Lord is your strength,"* said Nehemiah to Israel. In these days not many are so filled with the Spirit that they are charged with being drunk on new wine; not many act like a man intoxicated. Often a man under such an influence is liberal, willing to give the last cent away, but how much different they are from some of the professors of this age. When the

subject of tithing is brought up, they try to find some
excuse for not paying it or call it a subject of law.
What we need is Pentecostal experiences, then we
will have Pentecostal results. Our storehouses will
be full, and no commercial methods or begging will
be needed to continue the work of God. (6) As the
Romans, we should be **"full of goodness."** (Rom. 15:
14). This gives us the thought of benevolence. Although Christians are not saved by good works, they
will produce them after they are saved. What a
blessing good people are to a home, to the church,
and to a community. Oh, that we might have more
plain old-fashioned goodness! To be good to ourselves, good to our families, good to our church, and
good to our neighbors is our privilege if we are
where we should be in grace. (7) As the seven deacons, we should be **"full of wisdom."** (Acts 6:3).
This expresses the thought of soul-winning, *"He that
winneth souls is wise."* It requires wisdom to be a
soul-winner. The same method cannot be used in
dealing with various individual characters. It requires tact and sometimes righteous scheming to
bring some people to God. The word *"wisdom"* in
Acts 6:3 is from the Greek word **"sophia"** meaning
"skill." It was wisdom Jesus used in reaching the
woman at the well. How carefully He approached
her and gradually He revealed to her her lost state
and condition. There was nothing rude or unkind
in His manner of reaching the soul of this wayward
Samaritan. To the man who lacks this wisdom,
James urges him to ask of God, Who giveth to all
men liberally, (James 1:5), that he might be supplied with the patience which is so often required in

bringing men to Jesus Christ.

Notice the sevenfold list I have given you—full of the Holy Ghost, full of faith, full of glory, full of good works, full of new wine, full of goodness, and full of wisdom. All these are found in the New Testament and should be manifested in every Christian's life. As Paul, a Christian can say, **"I am full."** (Phil. 4:18). This speaks of an adequate supply, for in this chapter he reminds the Philippians of the provision and gifts sent by Epaphroditus to him in the Philippian jail. He declares, *"My God shall supply all your need."* (v. 19). This refers to spiritual as well as physical needs. After Jesus had fed the five thousand, the disciples took up the fragments that were left, and they found them to be twelve basketfuls, one basket for each apostle. It was a disgrace for a Jew to go to a Gentile for his provision. Likewise, God has provided each of us with a basketful of rich provisions (spiritually speaking) so that we need not go to the world and beg for any of our supplies in order to be spiritual people. Figuratively speaking, He provided us with a basketful of power, faith, glory, good works, new wine, goodness, and wisdom in order that we may say with Paul, *"I am full."* Naomi's confession was *"I went out full."* How many have gone out full of the above qualifications but have come back empty.

One profitable thought is seen in this lesson: she took the blame upon herself. She did not blame her deceased husband, her two boys, or the Lord, but she took the blame upon herself by saying, *"I went."* She got the "I" in its proper place. The responsibility came back on Naomi. How often a backslider will blame someone else for his downfall when in reality no one is to blame but himself. Often the cause can be traced back to days and months previous, to the hour of his breaking with God when he neglected secret prayer or failed to walk in the light.

She also acknowledged a blessed fact when she said, *"The Lord hath brought me home."* (v. 21). The **Lord,** the covenant God of Israel, had brought Naomi home. She called it **home.** Truly it is home to the backslider when he, like the prodigal son, returns. When the backslider gets back to prayer meeting, Christian fellowship, Bible Studies, and worship, he finds himself back home. A man in his own home may take special liberties. He may say, "Praise the Lord" or "Amen" right out loud when he feels like it because he is at home. The cupboard is always open to those at home; we have privileges at home we do not have elsewhere. So my advice is to stay at home. I have no objection to people visiting and enjoying the services of another church, but that can become such a practice that there will be no responsibility whatever. They finally become spiritual tramps, sometimes being forced to get their supplies from Moab's cupboard. I have often noticed when members of my congregation go elsewhere and neglect their own services, they come back with the confession that the services which they attended were very dead. The Lord brought them back empty, but the Spirit of the Lord visited our place of worship in a mighty way in the salvation of sinners, showering a special blessing upon the congregation. Let us consider—

C. THE SORROW IN WHICH SHE RETURN-

ED. Naomi's sorrow is expressed in the threefold confession which she makes to the inhabitants of Bethlehem. A confession without sorrow is not true repentance. Let us notice the threefold confession.

1. **"The Almighty hath dealt very bitterly with me."** (v. 20). The word *"bitter"* comes from the Hebrew word meaning "to embitter or make bitter." God had to get Naomi into a condition of soul bitterness before she would return. This was not a bitterness caused from unkind dealings of an earthly friend, but it was the chastising hand of God, shaping circumstances in Naomi's life, that caused her to see the folly of her way. She recognized the hand of the Almighty in it all.

2. **"The Lord hath testified against me."** (v. 21). The word **"testify"** is from the Hebrew word meaning *"to answer or respond."* According to Robert Young it is the same word found in Isaiah 59:12 where Isaiah in speaking to the Lord says, *"Our sins testify against us."* The same Lord Who brought her home was the Lord Who witnessed against her. When our lives are obedient and righteous in His sight, the manner in which He deals with us is the testimony that we are pleasing Him. It was so in the case of Abel, who offered *"a more excellent sacrifice than Cain, by which he obtained witness that he was righteous, God testifying of his gifts."* (Hebrews 11:4). So we see that God responded (which is the meaning of this word *"testify"*) to Naomi, but it was in a chastising manner.

3. **"The Almighty hath afflicted me."** (v. 21). The word *"afflicted"* means *"to do evil,"* as in the case of

Moses when he said, *"Wherefore hast thou afflicted thy servant?"* (Num. 11:11). The Lord has a method of dealing with His children and with backsliders, yea, even with sinners, to get them to a place where they are in subjection to Him. Sometimes the method is very severe; it may be loss of property, health, loved ones, or of reputation, but He has a way of afflicting mankind in the spirit of love to bring him unto Himself. So here we find God's dealings, God's testimony, and God's affliction against Naomi. Let us now study—

III. THE GRATIFYING SUPPLY.

As this couple journeyed to Bethlehem, they beheld the waving fields of barley, and they found that the message they had received in Moab was true— *"That the Lord had visited his people in giving them bread."* (Ruth 1:6). They would now have the opportunity to provide for themselves bread for the coming winter. Thus, it reminds us that there is a time to sow and a time to reap. If we would reap in the ages of eternity, we must sow in this dispensation of time. Let us note— (1) **She came back in the right manner.** This has been described under the division, *"A Grievous Sorrow."* (2) **She came back to the right place.** It was Bethlehem—the house of bread. If I desire to live in a warm climate, I must of necessity go where a warm climate prevails. Likewise, if I desire spiritual bread for my soul, I must go where spiritual bread may be obtained. The reason so many of God's people are living on half rations is because they are not willing to go to Bethlehem in the beginning of the barley harvest. Some of these

remain under the influence of modernistic teaching
or in a cold dead spiritual atmosphere while only a
few blocks from them is a spiritual place of worship
where their souls could be blessed and their testimonies would be welcomed. But rather than humble
themselves and worship with people who are less
popular and who have a more radical standard, they
prefer to die in Moab with the Laodicean worshipers.
God's plan for them is to come back to the right
place, and anything short of that will leave the soul
starving and in dire want.   (3) **She came back at
the right time.** *"In the beginning of the barley
harvest."* (Ruth 1:22). According to the Jewish Cal-
endar, that takes place in the spring of the Jewish
year. When a person reaches Bethlehem, it is springtime for his soul. The spiritual birds are singing; the
lilies-of-the-valley are blooming; the waving fields of
golden grain are testifying that it's harvest time.

It also speaks of joy. Isaiah writes of the joyful
worshipers. *"They joy before thee according to the
joy in harvest, and as men rejoice when they divide
the spoil."* (Isaiah 9:3). Jesus tells of the joy that
comes to the three classes of people when the lost
sheep is found. (Luke 15:3-7). First, the shepherd
rejoices, *"He layeth it on his shoulders, rejoicing."*
(v. 5). Then he calls his friends and neighbors together, typical of the church, and invites them to rejoice with him, for the sheep that was lost is found.
(v. 6). But he goes a step farther and says, *"Likewise,"* meaning just as Jesus and the Church rejoices
when a lost soul is found, "Heaven unites in rejoicing over the rescue." (v. 7). It also gives joy to the
sheep that is restored to the fold, for it knows that

now it is to be safely nestled on the shepherd's breast,
a place of affection; and to be supported by his shoulders, a place of strength. The barley harvest, which
indicates new life, is a producer of joy. It removes
the sorrows that were produced through a life of sin,
and it fills the spirit with holy joy and rapture.

THE BARLEY HARVEST

According to Exodus 9:31, 32, barley was the first
of the grain; flax was second; wheat was third. When
they arrived at Bethlehem in the beginning of the
barley harvest, it is evident that there was still more
to follow which is revealed in Ruth 2:23. This teaching leads us to deeper truths in grace which are
taught in the two divisions of the book—First, **"Find
Grace"**; Second, **"Find Rest."** There is a soul rest that
must be found by the believer; this is typical of the
wheat harvest. This subject will be treated later,
when we study chapter three.

The seven feasts of the Lord, which are recorded
in Leviticus 23, are as follows: (1) **The Feast of the
Passover.** (v. 5). This speaks of redemption, through
blood, from the land of Egypt, which is typical of our
redemption from a life of sin. The lamb slain points
forward to the Lamb of God, Jesus Christ. (2) **The
Feast of Unleavened Bread.** (v. 6). Leaven in the
Scripture is a type of evil and carnality and was not
to be used for holy purposes. (Ex. 12:15). Paul speaks
of it as malice and wickedness. (I Cor. 5:8). Leaven
removed from the bread gives the thought of separation, and it is also typical of a separated life in holy
communion with our Lord. (3) **The Feast of First-
fruits.** (v's. 9-14). This points forward to Jesus Christ,

the First-fruits of the resurrection of the dead. (I Cor. 15:22, 23). (4) **The Feast of Pentecost.** (v's. 15-22). This took place exactly fifty days after the feast of first-fruits. (v. 16). The two wave-loaves typify the union of the Jew and Gentile in the Church. They were made of fine flour, which speaks of the products of Calvary. The leaven within them denotes the sin or carnal life within the believer, which must pass through the purging and purifying process of the fire when the loaves were *"baken."* It was at this time, fifty days later than the barley harvest, that the full ingathering of summer grain and summer fruits occurred. How nicely God in Providence taught that the spring harvest brought to us the graces of justification but the more abundant harvest, a multiplied harvest of wheat (not barley), is received fifty days later in the baptism of the Holy Spirit. From this we see that Nature, Providence, and Scripture all picture the religious experience for the believer. (5) **The Feast of the Blowing of Trumpets.** (v's. 23-25). This occurred on the first day of the seventh month. The reader will note there was a great interval between the fourth feast, the feast of Pentecost, and the feast of trumpets. This is typical of the long interval of grace, this dispensation in which the Holy Spirit is gathering out the two loaves, the Jews and Gentiles, to form His Church. The feast of trumpets refers to the time when God will call Israel back to their own land, Palestine. Matthew speaks of the time when the *"angels with a great sound of a trumpet, shall gather together his elect from the four winds."* (Matt. 24: 31). Following that verse is the parable of the fig tree, teaching us that when the Jews take on new life as described here by "putting forth leaves, we should know that summer is nigh," or the time is at hand for the blowing of the trumpets. (6) **The Feast of Atonement.** (v's. 26-32). This is a time when reconciliation will be made between God and the Jewish people. *"They shall look upon me whom they have pierced, and they shall mourn for him . . . , and shall be in bitterness for him."* (Zech. 12:10). *"There shall be a fountain opened to the house of David and to the inhabitants of Jerusalem for sin and for uncleanness."* (Zech. 13:1). Thus, it shall be a national atonement; a nation shall be born in a day. (7) **The Feast of Tabernacles.** (v's. 33-43). The final feast of the Lord, which is to last seven days in the seventh month of the year, pictures the earthly millennial rest. Clarence Larkin has beautifully described this in the following words: "What the **'seventh day,'** or Sabbath, is to the week, a day of rest, so the **'seventh month'** to the other six months of the 'cycle,' typifies a period of rest—the **'Sabbatic Rest,'** of the **'Millennial Period'** in relation to the other six thousand years of the world's work day History." But you will notice that a holy convocation is to take place on the eighth day, and this gives us the thought of the new beginning when the new Heavens and earth will be ushered in, time and dispensations will have ceased, and we will be forever with the Lord. These seven feasts give us a prophetic picture in typical teaching of the plan of grace from the fall of man until the consummation of redemption when face to face we stand before the Redeemer in the unending age. Let us now go back to the feast of first-fruits and see how that is connected with the barley harvest.

The feast of first-fruits was the third of seven feasts. Three is typical of resurrection. *"As Jonas was three days and three nights in the whale's belly; so shall the Son of man be three days and three nights in the heart of the earth."* (Matt. 12:40). It, being the third feast, will give us resurrection truth. This feast marked the beginning of the harvest, announcing the death of winter. The cold winter with its severe winds and hardships is past, and spring has arrived. In the same way, Christ's resurrection announced the death of the old dispensation, the law and the beginning of the dispensation of grace. It announced that the law with its cruelty and sternness had passed, and grace had begun. Likewise, the resurrection life in the believer announces that his life of cruelty and sternness, winter with its cold hardships, is past, and new life, light, and love is now reigning in his being. A further proof that this feast speaks of resurrection is seen in the word *"first-fruits."* The very name given to the sheaf which was waved before the Lord is the name given to Him as the One *"risen from the dead"*—Christ, the First-fruits. (I Cor. 15:20). We notice in the study of the feasts of the Lord that the beginning of the barley harvest was marked by the waving of the sheaf of the first ripe grain, announcing the death of winter and the arrival of spring. Likewise is the beginning of this church age, which is marked by the resurrection of the Lord Jesus Christ. It is springtime to the soul to every one who is risen with Christ and is made partaker of His Divine life. This sheaf was to be waved in the land *"which I give unto you,"* says the Lord. (Lev. 23:10). This land of Canaan was the land of plenty. The Lord called it *"a good land, a land of brooks of water, of fountains and depths that spring out of valleys and hills; A land of wheat, and barley, and vines, and fig trees, and pomegranates; a land of oil olive, and honey; A land wherein thou shalt eat bread without scarceness, thou shalt not lack any thing in it; a land whose stones are iron, and out of whose hills thou mayest dig brass."* (Deut. 8:7-9). It was a land in which they should lack nothing. In the same way, the believer who enters on resurrection territory should lack nothing. He can say with Paul of old, *"Christ is all"*—all he has and all he needs is found in Christ. His pardon, his union, his new life, his joy, and new desires all come through Jesus, but the **claims of Jehovah** must first be recognized in obtaining all this prosperity and blessing. God must come first in the believer's life. This is found in Leviticus 23 verse 14 where it reads, *"Ye shall eat neither bread, nor parched corn, nor green ears, until the self-same day that ye have brought an offering unto your God."* If we will remember God first, we can have the parched corn and the green ears in abundance.

By the waving of this sheaf, it was also a pledge to Israel that many sheaves were to follow, a type and foreshadowing of a future resurrection in which the saints who die in the Lord rise and go forth to meet Christ. Moreover, every Naomi and Ruth of this present dispensation that come back to the Father's house will come (spiritually speaking) in the beginning of the barley harvest. There every Christian will find a Gracious Supply—a supply of forgiveness, of life, of peace, of joy—in fact all that he needs for body, soul, and spirit.   Although in the Book of Ruth there's no suggestion to the cross of Christ, yet it lacks no hint that leads us to the blessed truth of death and resurrection.   This hint is found in the words *"in the beginning of the barley harvest."* There could be no harvest of grain without the death of the kernel, neither can there be any resurrection without the crucifixion.   This study concludes the first chapter of the Book, the main thought being Naomi's affliction.   Our next study will enter into the thought of Ruth's activity.

THE DAMSEL AND THE RELATIONSHIP

STUDY FOUR

(Ruth 2:1-14)

In this study, we find Naomi, the backslider, blessedly restored to Bethlehem-judah. Ruth, the Gentile sinner, is also safely gathered with the Israelites of God. Both have been tested, but through it they have proved that God was to come first and foremost in their lives. Orpah is entirely out of the picture. She remains in Moab with her relatives and her religion. Many, like her, have failed to take the way God has outlined in His Word. From now on, Ruth moves forward in activity, advancement, and alliance and seems to surpass Naomi in prominency. This portrays the Jew, who is set aside temporarily so that the Gentiles might be partakers of Divine grace. Another character is now introduced for the first time in the Book; his name is Boaz. In our present lesson we will see—

> I. **RUTH'S WORK.**
> II. **RUTH'S WELCOME.**
> III. **RUTH'S WEALTH.**

I. RUTH'S WORK.

In chapter two we are introduced for the first time to the near kinsman, one who has the right to redeem. Boaz was a *"mighty man"* and a *"man of wealth."* His name means *"in him is strength."* In Ruth's first day of new life, she meets Boaz, the one who is able to redeem. How beautifully this portrays a converted man coming in contact with Jesus Christ. A man is not saved unless he becomes a partaker of

the mighty power of the Savior. The zeal in the
new life of the convert can be plainly seen in Ruth's
ambition to glean. (chapter 2:2).

There is a threefold request in this chapter, which
is as follows: (1) **"Let me go."** (v. 2). This splendid
ambition is often seen in the new convert. (2) **"Let
me glean."** (v. 7). Not only does a new convert desire to go and do something for God and His work,
but he desires to glean in the Word of God and find
that which will satisfy his soul. (3) **"Let me find."**
(v. 13). What a righteous desire! She wants to find
favor in the sight of her Lord. She is seeking the
smiles and blessings of Him Who alone is able to
bestow. The spirit of humility and dependency is
seen in Ruth as she seeks from Naomi, the elder
woman, permission to go and glean in the field for
ears of corn. She seeks counsel from one who is
older in experience. This shows a beautiful spirit.
A new convert who is heady and high-minded will
make a poor Christian, for all, either young or old,
are more or less dependent upon one another. We
are all in need of fellowship, counsel, encouragement, and advice; and the heady, high-minded believer will sooner or later learn for his own good that
what he can gain from the older Christian is worth
much to his experience. Let us note—

A. A SPECIAL PROVISION FOR GENTILES.
B. A SUCCESSFUL PLACE TO GLEAN.
C. A SPLENDID PICTURE OF GRACE.
A. A SPECIAL PROVISION FOR GENTILES.

The term *"Ruth, the Moabitess,"* is found five times
in the Book. Chaps. 1:22; 2:2, 21; 4:5, 10. She is here

identified with the idolatrous worshipers of Moab. They were forbidden to come into the congregation of the Lord even up to the tenth generation. Thus, we see she was a stranger to the covenants of promise. (Eph. 2:12). She is here a representative of the Gentile sinner.

THE NUMBER FIVE

Why is the word *"Moabitess"* found just five times? The number five in Scripture speaks of grace. When Israel marched out of Egypt, they marched out five in a rank, (Ex. 13:18, margin), showing they were delivered on the grounds of grace. When David went to meet Goliath, the giant, he took five stones from the brook and his sling as his weapon. Some say, "But he needed only one stone to slay the giant." This is true. There were four stones left, which show that there is always grace left to help us for the next time of need. The holy anointing oil was composed of five ingredients and took on the name of pure anointing oil, speaking of pure grace. (Ex. 30:23, 24). The brazen altar was five cubits square, which pictures the grace of the Lord Jesus Christ in giving His life a ransom for lost men. In feeding the multitudes, Jesus took five barley loaves, typical of weakness, and fed five thousand people, showing that by Divine grace He could feed many, and sufficient was the remainder to supply each disciple with a basketful for his journey. This portrayed the imparting of His grace to multitudes in the dispensation of the Holy Spirit.

The term *"Moab"* is found eight times in the Book. In a preceding study, I explained that eight was the number of a new beginning. From this we see Moab, typical of the Gentile race, was to have a new beginning on the grounds of grace. The term *"Moabitish"* is found but once in the Book. This completes the perfect number, for the word *"Moab"* is found eight times, the term "Moabitess" is found five times, and *"Moabitish"* once, making a total of 14, $2\times7=14$. Thus, we have a twofold dispensational perfection.

Let us notice the special provision provided for strangers, the Gentiles. In chapter three the seven feasts of the Lord, (Leviticus 23), were described. Verses 15 to 21 deal with the feast of Pentecost. At this time the wheat harvest, which occurred about fifty days later than the barley harvest, was at its height. Verse 22 tells of the special provisions made at this particular time for the poor and the strangers. The verse reads as follows: *"And when ye reap the harvest of your land, thou shalt not make clean riddance of the corners of thy field when thou reapest, neither shalt thou gather any gleaning of thy harvest: thou shalt leave them unto the poor, and to the stranger: I am the Lord your God."* From a dispensational aspect, the poor and strangers could be none others than the Gentiles for whom these special provisions were provided. That God should order the Israelites not to make clean riddance of the corners of their fields or gather the gleaning of the harvest so that the stranger might have supplies that will care for them until the next feast, which occurred in the seventh month, is a provision of grace. How nicely this points forward to this age when we Gentiles may eat the crumbs which fall from the Master's table. According to the Syrophenician woman, (Matt. 15:22-28), the crumbs or the gleanings of grace are sufficient for the satisfaction of the soul.

Let us carry this study into Deuteronomy 24:19-22. There we read as follows: *"When thou cuttest down thine harvest in thy field, and hast forgot a sheaf in the field, thou shalt not go again to fetch it: it shall be for the stranger, for the fatherless, and for the widow: that the Lord thy God may bless thee in all the work of thine hands. When thou beatest thine olive trees, thou shalt not go over the boughs again: it shall be for the stranger, for the fatherless, and for the widow. When thou gatherest the grapes of thy vineyard, thou shalt not glean it afterward: it shall be for the stranger, for the fatherless, and for the widow. And thou shalt remember that thou wast a bondman in the land of Egypt: therefore I command thee to do this thing."* In these verses we notice three classes of people—the stranger, the fatherless, and the widow— and three articles of provision—wheat from the sheaf, oil from the olive, and wine from the grapes. If they forgot a sheaf in the field, they were to leave it there that the stranger, the fatherless, and the widow might have that for their portion. The wheat gives us the thought of flour, which is made into the bread of life. This represents Christ, Who declared, *"I am the bread of life."* The second item was oil from the olive. When they shook the olive trees, some of the olives remained upon their branches. These they were to leave for the stranger, the fatherless, and the widow that they might enjoy the luxury of olive oil, which at that time was eaten with other food. This is typical of the Holy Spirit as it is pictured in Matthew 25:

1-10 where the foolish virgins failed to provide themselves with oil. Therefore, God has provided that the strangers (Gentiles) may have a large supply of the holy anointing oil in and upon their lives. Third, let us notice that they were not to glean their vineyards, but they were to leave all unripened grapes that they might ripen, thus providing for the stranger, the fatherless, and the widow, grapes for wine, typical of joy.

Notice them in their order. How wonderfully it portrays the inspiration of Scripture. Life is the first thing needed, and it is the first thing offered. (v. 19). Second in order is the olive oil, which speaks of the spirit of power. Bread (life) was provided in the crucifixion and resurrection of Christ, but fifty days later the Holy Spirit was poured out on the day of Pentecost, supplying spiritual blessings (wine) for the Church of the living God. This truth is also taught in the cleansing of the leper. When the blood, representing life, was applied to the right ear, the right thumb, and the great toe of the right foot, it pointed forward to the life that Christ was to give as a ransom for polluted lepers. Then followed the oil. The priest would take a log of oil, pour it into the palm of his left hand, and sprinkle it seven times before the Lord, giving the leper a perfect standing in God's sight. Then he would take the oil and cover the blood on the tip of the right ear, upon the thumb of the right hand, and upon the great toe of the right foot, and the remainder he would pour upon the head of the cleansed leper. After the blood and oil had been applied, the leper was cleansed in God's sight, but the remainder of the oil poured on the head was typical of constant anointings along the way every Christian needs from time to time. (Nui 12-18). Thus, we see here life in blood, power i oil, and joy and blessings in the wine for the cleansed leper (typical of sinners) when he was admitted into the camp and was permitted to have fellowship and joy with the Israelites of God. How wonderful these Old Testament studies portray the New Testament plan of grace.

Let us notice the three classes we have previously mentioned, namely, the strangers, the fatherless, and the widows. **First,** the strangers referred to those outside of the covenant of Israel, the Gentile nations. **Second,** there were the fatherless. This class must refer to none other in the spiritual realm than the backslider, for *"fatherless"* speaks of two things, birth, and death. It is the same in the spiritual realm; it refers to those who once enjoyed grace from the hand of God but now do not enjoy it. **Third,** the widow is mentioned. This refers to Israel, not as a nation but to the individual Jews of which the nation is composed. Israel is now in widowhood according to Romans 7:1, 2. Although, as a nation, Israel has been temporarily cast off, there are still provisions made for the individual Jew who may desire life, power, and joy. Let us note—

B. A SUCCESSFUL PLACE TO GLEAN. Her holy desire to glean is found in chapter 2:2 where she says, *"Let me now go."* Her gleaning she would not put off for another time. Her desire was to be busy at once. How this marks the picture of a new-born soul desiring after Divine Truth and gleaning ears of corn from the Word of God. How natural it is for a newly-converted soul to want others to find the same peace and joy he is experiencing, and how many of us, when we were saved, thought our whole family, neighbors, and friends would at once seek the same salvation, but to our disappointment we found they rejected the same Christ that we had previously rejected. A beautiful truth is seen when she requests to be allowed to *"glean ears of corn after him."* Anyone who will glean after Christ is sure to get corn. Corn is not found in the funny-page of your daily paper, in many of the magazines found on library tables, or in novels often read by so-called Christians. If the Christian wants corn, he will have to find it in the Word of God and in good religious books or periodicals. Glean after Christ, and you will have, as the disciples after the feeding of the multitudes, a basketful to carry with you.

C. A SPLENDID PICTURE OF GRACE. *"And she went, and came, and gleaned in the field after the reapers: and her hap was to light on a part of the field belonging unto Boaz, who was of the kindred of Elimelech."* (v. 3). One writer says, "The word field was in the singular because there were no fences marking off fields." Stones were used to mark the boundary of their land. In Proverbs 22:28 we read: *"Remove not the ancient landmark,* (or stone markers), *which thy fathers have set."* These were the landmarks that showed the divisions of the fields, the same as fences today. There was an instruction given to Israel in Deuteronomy 19:14: *"Thou shalt not remove thy neighbour's landmark,"* and a curse was pronounced upon the man that did so. (Deut. 27:17).

It was God's special plan of grace that she should begin her gleaning on the territory that belonged to him who was later to be her husband. Today, God, by a special plan of Providence, arranges that a tract should fall into the right party's hand, that he should move into a certain neighborhood, or that he, out of curiosity, would attend a camp meeting, or Bible conference and thereby, as Ruth, come into the field of Boaz. How wonderfully Providence has led men from time to time until they came to the right place to find God. Seemingly God arranges man's salvation at an appointed time, in an appointed way, and at an appointed place. It isn't guesswork. God has His eye on man from the cradle to the grave.

Let us notice the demand of Solomon, *"Remove not the ancient landmarks."* There are four landmarks in the field of Christ. If these are removed, a man will no longer be in the territory of grace but in the districts of sin. These four cornerstones or landmarks are incarnation, crucifixion, resurrection, and ascension. If a person will remain within this boundary and glean, he will find ears of corn that will feed his soul and encourage him to press on to higher heights and deeper depths in God. The same instruction that Boaz gave to Ruth, Christ gives to us, *"Go not to glean in another field, neither go from hence."* (v. 8). If one will stay within the fundamental doctrines of Christ, he will find plenty of gleanings along the way.

II. RUTH'S WELCOME.

In our study today we find the following alliteration:

1. THE GLEANINGS OF RUTH.
2. THE GREETINGS OF THE REAPERS.
3. THE GRACE OF THE REDEEMER.

In the fourth verse (second chapter), we find Boaz greeting the reapers; this is in the form of a blessing: *"The Lord be with you."* To this the reapers reply, *"The Lord bless thee."* In those days that was the established custom of greeting between employer and employee. What a wonderful world this would be if that relationship would exist today between masters and their servants, but we will have to wait a few more years until the Millennial Age when such blessedness shall exist. The gulf is becoming larger and larger between capital and labor until strikes are known throughout the universe. James pictures very forcefully this condition for the last days and urges the Christian brethren to be patient unto the coming of the Lord. (James 5:7). He uses Job as an illustration of a man of patience.

Boaz at once notices the newcomer in his congregation, and he asks, *"Whose damsel is this?"* (Ruth 2:5). He desires to know all the gleaners in his field. The servant replies that it is the Moabitish damsel that came back with Naomi out of the land of Moab. (v. 6). He further tells Boaz how she requested permission to glean in the field and how she had continued to do so until the present time when they were gathered **into the house.** I want to call your attention to the words *"in the house,"* for it gives us a new line of truth, commonly known as *"church truth."* We notice Jesus used a different line of teaching when by the seashore than He did in the house. One seemed to be for the world at large and the other for the disciples or those who were following Him. So the next verses in our study give us some thoughts for the believer of which Ruth is here typical. This fact is seen in the way Boaz addresses Ruth. She is no longer called *"the damsel,"* but he calls her *"my daughter."* (v. 8). Ruth is pictured in this study in the following threefold relationship:

1. A DAMSEL IN THE FIELD. (v's. 1-6).
2. A DAUGHTER IN THE HOUSE. (v's. 7-13).
3. A DINER AT THE TABLE. (v. 14).

When Boaz called her *"my daughter,"* she received a welcome from him. In the same way, our Heavenly Boaz (Jesus) will welcome all who come to Him and will give them the titles of *"sons"* and *"daughters,"* which refer to sonship through the new birth in Jesus Christ. I desire to give a little practical truth here for the Church. A welcome to sinners in the house of God may be the means of many finding Christ. Often strangers who visit the house of the Lord must sit there without a song book to sing from and must leave without a hand shake or a word of welcome from anyone. In some places, the members instead will clique together and enjoy the fellowship of each other while the sinner passes out without an invitation to return or without feeling that anyone is concerned regarding his presence. This same situation exists in camp meetings; believers come to have their souls fed, but receive no welcome and are treated as strangers while on the grounds. In my early Christian life I attended meetings to which I felt I would never want to return because I received no welcome. Let us, as Christians, be careful regarding this particular matter.

THE UNNAMED SERVANT

I wish to call your attention to the **unnamed servant,** *"that was set over the reapers."* (v. 6). It does not tell who this servant was. Some may wonder why he, who has such an important part in the work of Boaz and who carried the responsibility of the reapers and the managing of his fields, is not named, but this is made plain if viewed from a dispensational standpoint. The Holy Spirit is the unnamed servant of the dispensation of grace. He was without a name that He might exalt a name which is above every name; that name is Jesus. There are three characters in the Old Testament whose servants were unnamed. They are given as follows in their typical order: **First,** Abraham sent forth his *"eldest servant,"* (Gen. 24:2), into the far-off country to seek a bride for Isaac; the servant's name is not mentioned, but it states *"that he ruled over all that he had."* (v. 2). Here we see a picture of the Holy Spirit coming into the far-off country, this world of sin, to call out a bride for the Heavenly Isaac, Jesus. The Holy Spirit is now engaged in this work. **Second,** there is Boaz, whose unnamed servant had charge *"over the reapers."* (Ruth 2:6). This is typical of the Holy Spirit bestowing His gifts upon those who are engaged in the vineyard of the Lord as gleaners and reapers of the harvest. **Third,** we find in the case of Joseph, who was a type of Jesus Christ. When the brethren of Joseph brought Benjamin to him he gave special instruction to the *"ruler of his house,"* (Gen. 43:16) saying, *"Bring these men*

*home, and slay, and make ready; for these men shall
dine with me at noon. And the man did as Joseph
bade; and the man brought the men into Joseph's
house."* (Gen. 43:16, 17). It was the ruler of his
house, the unnamed servant, who brought these men
home that they might dine with their brother Joseph
at his table. In like manner, the Holy Spirit is busily
engaged bringing the redeemed of the earth to their
Heavenly home that they might dine with their elder
Brother, Jesus, at the marriage of the Lamb. Thus,
we have the work of the Holy Spirit revealed in a
threefold manner: first, how He came to call men out
of the world of sin to a life of righteousness, then how
He bestows upon them His gifts and graces, and pre-
pares them for the marriage supper of the Lamb.
This truth is blessedly portrayed in the servant of
Boaz, who is a type of the Holy Ghost bringing Ruth
into the house, a type of the Church of God. From
this we see the typical teaching of the Holy Spirit is
not left out of this little Book of Ruth, which so re-
markably portrays the dispensation of grace. Let us
notice four facts relative to Christian life:

A. GOOD INSTRUCTIONS. *"Go not to glean
in another field, neither go from hence, but abide here
fast by my maidens."* (v. 8). Boaz opens the conversation by saying, *"Hearest thou not, my daughter?"*
He requested that she give him her attention, then he
gave the following instructions: **1st,** *"Go not to
glean in another field."* This was special instruction to
remain separate; he asked her not to run off to the
world for her supply but to remain by his maidens. A
continuous separation for the believer is demanded

by God. Seemingly this is the first instruction that Ruth receives. Some may wonder why this is so important that it should come first, but Jesus in His high priestly prayer said, *"The world hath hated them, because they are not of the world, even as I am not of the world."* (John 17:14). In His address on the vine and the branches, He said to His disciples, *"If the world hate you, ye know that it hated me before it hated you. If ye were of the world, the world would love his own: but because ye are not of the world, but I have chosen you out of the world, therefore the world hateth you."* (John 15:18, 19). It is the world that crucified and is now rejecting Christ, and when the Church becomes allied with it, it will soon lose its spiritual power, as Samson of old, who fell into the lap of Delilah, typical of the world. **2nd,** she was instructed to cherish Christian fellowship, *"Abide here fast by my maidens."* (v. 8). It is not enough to remain separate, but man should cherish Christian fellowship, for that is comfort for the soul. The older maidens, who had the advantage of longer experience and who were more accustomed to the work in the field of Boaz, would be desirable companions for her, for they could direct her rightly. It is advisable for any new convert to keep close to the older established Christian that he might learn to walk in the paths of righteousness for His name's sake. Boaz adds, *"Let thine eyes be on the field."* Special instruction is given here concerning the **eyes,** for a glance into the field of the world might cause an unlawful desire, which might later prove a disaster as in the case of Eve, who looked upon the fruit and ere long ate of the forbidden product.

B.   GREAT   PROVISIONS.   **1st,**   he   provided

protection, *"Have I not charged the young men that they shall not touch thee?"* (v. 9). As long as we stay in the field of our Heavenly Boaz, we are under His protection; under the shadow of His wing, there is perfect security; and it is under the wings of the Almighty that she had come to trust. (v. 12). What a blessed place of retreat! I was recently told of an aged Christian man of splendid character. One night he was returning at a late hour to his home. As he, with no sense of danger, was hurriedly crossing the street, a strong hand forcibly pushed him backward, thus halting him on his onward course. The force of the assault was so strong it nearly pushed him over, and in the next second an automobile came dashing by at a rapid rate of speed. Immediately he looked for the stranger, whom he thought had severely pushed him to stop him from rushing into the path of the on-coming car, but to his amazement no one was to be seen. He looked to the right and left, but there was no one around. Who was it then? It was the hand of the Divine, Who was interested in His own child, and in mercy spared his life for a few more months or years so that he could fulfill his work on this earth. This incident actually occurred in the State of California. It illustrates the hand of God in protection.

2nd, she received restoration, *"When thou art athirst, go unto the vessels, and drink of that which the young men have drawn."* (v. 9). A good drink from the wells of salvation restores the weary gleaners in their efforts of service as they glean in the field of Boaz. He said, *"Drink of that which the young men have drawn."* The young preachers and workers are

able today to draw from the wells of truth, and they
are able to give the Christian that which will aid him
in his spiritual activity. With Boaz these young men
"draw water out of the wells of salvation." Notice
the liberty he gave to Ruth, *"when thou art athirst,
go unto the vessels."* Any time, any place, and in any
condition, Christ invites us to drink.

C. GLORIOUS ADORATION. *"Then she fell on
her face, and bowed herself to the ground."* (v. 10).
With such instruction and wonderful provision, she is
immediately struck with a spirit of humility and deep
reverence.   She bows in adoration and questions,
" 'Why have I found grace in thine eyes?' I am only
a stranger; how is it that you have given me, a Moabitess, so much? Pray tell me, why have you extended
to me such wonderful grace?" How many of God's
people today have experienced this same feeling when
they see the marvels of His grace—how they have
been redeemed, forgiven of all the past sin, washed
in His blood, filled with His Spirit, are now enjoying
Christian fellowship, and possessing a blessed pros-
pect for the future. We ask ourselves the question,
"Why have we found grace in His sight?" What a
touching thought she expressed when she classed
herself as a stranger, an outcast of Israel, and an idol-
ater of Moab. Such were we Gentiles before we were
saved. Boaz answers her question by saying, *"It hath
fully been shewed me, all that thou hast done."* (v.
11). **1st**, he speaks of her separation, *"How thou
hast left thy father and thy mother, and the land of
thy nativity."* (v. 11). Boaz recognized the separation she made when she left her relatives and her re-

ligion as mentioned in chapter one. Two of the hardest things in the world for people to do is to leave their relatives and to leave their religions. Boaz fully knew all that she had done and, likewise, our Heavenly Boaz understands the decisions and desires of each heart. **2nd,** he mentions the acceptance, *"Art come unto a people which thou knewest not heretofore."* (v. 11). She had become a Jewish proselyte. To accept meant not only to renounce her own relatives and religions but also to embrace the people of another race and of another faith—to renounce the old and to take on the new.

D. GRACIOUS RECOMPENCE. *"A full reward be given thee."* (v. 12). She has a promise of a full reward. Some will receive but a partial reward, some will receive no reward at all, but Ruth had a promise of a *"full reward."* This reward is to come from the Lord God of Israel. It was not man's reward, for he cannot reward honestly and justly; he can only look upon the surface, but the Lord, Who understands the motives back of each life and act, will reward not according to our success but according to our faithfulness.

Doctor Watson, the great Methodist writer, in his book, *"Our Own God,"* pens the following wonderful words concerning rewards: "So many times our dear Savior uses the word 'great' in connection with coming rewards, so that for a few sufferings, for a few tears, for a few toils, which in reality are essential to our own welfare, Jesus says 'great is your reward in heaven.' It looks as if God was beside Himself in love for us. Just see, out of His love He gave us this wonderful existence, and then gave us grace to repent, to believe, and to love Him in return, and out of His love gave us the sanctifying Spirit, to live and labor for Him; and then out of His love He contrives to reward us, with honors, and glories in the age to come. He gives us the love to love Him with, and then rewards us for loving Him with His own love. Did you ever see the beat of it in all the world? If we pondered these things, would not our hearts burn within us, with a feverish desire to love Him up to all our capacity?"

III. RUTH'S WEALTH.

Under the division "Ruth's Work," we have seen Ruth as a **damsel** in the field. Under the division, "Ruth's Welcome," she was pictured as a **daughter** in the house. Under this division, "Ruth's Wealth," we shall see her as a **diner** at the table. From this it is evident that grace not only bestows new life, relationship, fellowship, and blessing, but it also provides the opportunity to gain rewards. Let us note—

A. THE ACKNOWLEDGMENT. *"Thou hast comforted me, and for that thou hast spoken friendly unto thine handmaid."* (v. 13). She was so charmed with her first day with Boaz, with the fellowship, promises, and blessings he gave that she was forced to acknowledge, *"I find favour in thy sight."* (v. 13, margin). The word *"favour"* is from the Hebrew word *"chen"* and is the same Hebrew word as *"grace"* found in chapter two, verse ten. She acknowledges she has found grace in the sight of Boaz, and says,

"Thou hast comforted me." The words of Boaz were
words of comfort; they were like honey to the taste,
like incense to the nostrils, like music to the ear, and
like scenery to the eye. His words were not only
comforting but charming. How wonderfully Christ
can speak words of welcome, forgiveness, friendship,
and encouragement! He knows just when and where
we need them most. She goes one step further in her
acknowledgment and says, *"Thou hast spoken to the
heart of thine handmaid."* (v. 13, margin). Christ not
only speaks to the ear, but His words of comfort find
lodgment in the heart. The religion of Jesus Christ
is a heart religion. While many today are training
the physical, Christ trains the heart. Then her acknowledgment is consummated with a spirit of humility, *"Though I be not like unto one of thine handmaidens."* She felt herself the least among the thousands of Bethlehem-judah, and yet out of her was to
come the ruler in Israel. (Micah 5:2). The New
Testament quotation, *"He that humbleth himself
shall be exalted,"* is fulfilled in Ruth. What an acknowledgment she had given: first, a favor extended;
second, a comfort received; third, words rightly
spoken; and fourth, the least among the thousands of
Judah.

B. THE INVITATION. The previous acknowledgment of Ruth so stirred the heart of Boaz in affection for her that he adds more grace, more comfort, and gives her a special invitation to dine. She
has an invitation to the table of the Lord. Now we
see the convert rising higher in Divine grace until she
is now a partaker of Divine ordinance. Boaz says,
"At mealtime come thou hither, and eat of the bread,

and dip thy morsel in the vinegar." (v. 14). The provisions on the table were bread and vinegar. The
word *"vinegar"* is from the Hebrew word *"chomets,"*
which is the word used for sour grapes or grapes that
have been made into sour wine. From this we see the
elements of the table are bread and wine, thus pointing forward to the dispensation of grace in which we
are living. (The Book of Ruth is full of dispensational
teaching.) She is now invited to partake of sweet
fellowship that she might have the opportunity to express her appreciation of the bread, the body that was
broken, and the wine, the blood that was shed. This
points forward to another table found in II Samuel 9.
Saul, who mightily opposed David on his march to
the throne, had a descendant by the name of Mephibosheth. David invited him to sit at his table, which
foreshadowed an act of Divine grace. This invitation
so affected Mephibosheth that he fell on his face and
did reverence. (II Sam. 9:6). As Ruth, he said, *"What
is thy servant, that thou shouldest look upon such a
dead dog as I am?"* (II Sam. 9:8). All who are invited to the table of the Lord also feel that they are
not worthy to be partakers; it is only by Divine grace
that we receive the invitation. Mephibosheth, who
represents the sinner, was so affected by the fall of
man that he was unable to produce a righteous walk,
being lame in both feet. However, while the emblem-
atic elements of the atonement, bread and wine,
were on the table, he was able to sit there in peace.
In the same way, man today may enjoy the communion at the Lord's table in peace and gratitude because
of what Christ has accomplished for him and in him
by His atonement. How much like Mephibosheth

are the children of light. Although they have been
forgiven of all transgressions and their hearts have
been made pure by the blood of the Lamb, yet because of poor judgment, human mistakes are made,
which in a measure affect the walk of life. Nevertheless, we have a place where our feet are covered
by Divine atonement; that is under the Lord's table.
We will close this study with the thought of—

C. THE SUFFICIENCY. *"She sat beside the
reapers."* (v. 14). The weary gleaner not only needs
nourishment, but he needs rest. To meet this need
she was privileged to sit beside the reapers. Food and
rest must go together, and so unlike the beast of the
field, who eats standing, we are provided with a place
to sit. **Sitting** in the Scripture always indicates a work
accomplished. After the demoniac had been delivered
from the legion of devils, we find him no longer
among the tombs living a life of self-destruction but
rather calmly *"sitting at the feet of Jesus, clothed,
and in his right mind."* (Luke 8:35). His posture indicated a work accomplished. The same truth is found
in the Book of Hebrews, which deals with the New
Testament High Priest. In four different places in this
Epistle, you will find some form of the verbs *"sit"* or
"set": Chap. 1:3; Chap. 8:1; Chap. 10:11, 12; Chap.
12:2. The writer in this Epistle is exalting Jesus
Christ above the Levitical priesthood and the other
various Old Testament characters by describing Him
"sitting down on the right hand of God"—with a work
accomplished—in a place of honor. There was no seat
provided for the priest in the Tabernacle because his
work was never completed; Israel's sins were not en-

tirely removed, and sacrifices had to be made continually because of constant transgression. The high priest entered into the Holy of Holies once a year, according to Hebrews 9:7, to put away the sin and transgression of the past year, but the writer to the Hebrews said, *"This man (Jesus) after he had offered one sacrifice for sins for ever, sat down on the right hand of God."* (Chap. 10:12). He emphasized that the High Priest was a man, *"this man."* Now we have, as our High Priest, perfect manhood sitting in the seat of intercession on the right hand of God. This indicates the accomplished work of atonement. It is completed. What man or God could add to it would be valueless. When we find Ruth sitting beside the reapers, it indicates, from a spiritual standpoint, that atonement had been accomplished in her life in the work of regeneration.

You will notice that while she sat at the table, Boaz *"reached her parched corn."* (v. 14). Parched corn has a wonderful significance in the work of redemption accomplished in and by Jesus Christ. S. Ridout writes: "She gets food from his own hand. The heart of our Lord is not satisfied till He Himself is ministering to the soul. How He longs for this personal contact, not satisfied merely with feeding, but passing the food from His own hand to the needy one." How true this is. There is a threefold lesson concerning Jesus Christ, typified by the corn. (1) The corn of wheat, ground into fine flour, as seen in the meat offering of Leviticus 2, pictures the Lord in His incarnation and earthly life. The grinding of the corn into the flour speaks of the suffering which He endured during His earthly career. *"Yet it pleased the Lord to bruise him."* (Isaiah 53:10). The corn must pass through the grinding process before it could be made into fine flour. In the same way nearly the whole life of Christ was one of suffering and sorrow. (2) The corn was parched. This speaks of the crucifixion of Christ, how He passed through the fiery judgments of Calvary. Jesus brings out this thought when He says, *"Except a corn of wheat fall into the ground and die, it abideth alone."* (John 12:24). The fire must pass over the corn to parch it. This reminds us that we are bought with a price; that price was the suffering, death, and penalty that He bore. He, Who knew no sin, was made sin. He endured the cross, despised the shame, took upon Himself the penalty that mankind deserved, explored death's chambers, endured its agony, and conquered its destinies. All this truth is seen in the parched corn. (3) The corn also speaks of resurrection. When the children of Israel came to Gilgal in the land of Canaan, they did eat of the old corn of the land and the parched corn the very day that they entered. (Josh. 5:11). The old corn here speaks of Christ in His incarnation as the Son of God, the parched corn speaks of crucifixion as just stated, but the eating speaks of Christ in resurrection, which is proven in Leviticus 23. We again refer to the feast of the Lord, where God demanded that on entering Canaan's land they should wave a sheaf of the first-fruits of their harvest before the priest and bring an offering after which they were allowed to eat parched corn, as has been explained. This feast was the feast which was typical of resurrection. When Boaz handed to Ruth this corn, he imparted to her this threefold truth on which she could feed, namely, His incarnation, His crucifixion, and His resurrection. What sacred food for the saints of God, who feed at His table in holy fellowship! They do not feed on what the world offers or on human emotion but on Christ, Who is all and in all. You will notice the closing words of this study: *"And she did eat, and was sufficed, and left."* (Ruth 2:14). The word *"sufficed"* means *"she was satisfied,"* which also Ruth's name indicates. There can be no satisfaction for the soul unless it is found in Jesus Christ. He alone can meet all the needs of the human heart. We are closing this study with Ruth in a state of satisfaction.

If the reader desires, he may use the following outline, dealing with the kinsman redeemer, in studying chapter 2:1-14. Note the kinsman's—(1) **Inquiry.** *"Whose damsel is this?"* (v. 5). (2) **Interview.** *"Hearest thou not, my daughter?"* (v. 8). (3) **Instruction.** *"Go not to glean in another field, neither go from hence, but abide here fast by my maidens."* (v. 8). (4) **Interest.** *"Have I not charged the young men that they shall not touch thee? and when thou art athirst, go unto the vessels, and drink."* (v. 9). (5) **Information.** *"It hath fully been shewed me, all that thou hast done unto thy mother-in-law since the death of thine husband: and how thou hast left thy father and thy mother, and the land of thy nativity, and art come unto a people which thou knewest not heretofore."* (v. 11). (6) **Invocation.** *"The Lord recompense thy work, and a full reward be given thee of the Lord God of Israel."* (v. 12). (7) **Invitation.** *"At*

*mealtime come thou hither, and eat of the bread, and
dip thy morsel in the vinegar."* (v. 14).

THE DEMAND AND THE REVELATION

STUDY FIVE

(Chap. 2:15-23.)

The last word in our last study was *"left."* Having been provided with rest and nourishment at the table of Boaz, she now proceeds to her day's work of gleaning. After we have received rest and nourishment, it is always easier to work than it was before. That is just what grace does. Jesus said, *"Come unto me . . . and I will give you rest."* He provides rest for the soul and then says, *"Follow me, and I will make you fishers of men."* As the law said, *"Work and then rest,"* they were provided in that dispensation with rest at the close of the week by keeping the Sabbath. On the other hand, under grace (of which this lesson is typical) we are provided with soul rest through the resurrection of Christ. Thus, we keep Sunday, the first day of the week, as a day of worship and then proceed to work the balance of the week to show our gratitude for the rest that was provided. It says she *"left."* It must have been a cross for her to leave such a place as that—a place where she had been resting with the reapers at the table of fellowship, receiving parched corn, bread and wine, the emblems of Christ's death and suffering. Truly, it must have been as hard for Ruth to leave the table of Boaz as it was for Peter, James, and John to leave the Mount of Transfiguration. Peter was so enraptured there that he said, *"Let us build three tabernacles"* because he wanted to remain there permanently. However, Jesus had another work to perform. He must tread down the Mount of Transfiguration into the valley of

Gethsemane and up to the Mount of Golgotha, there
to die for a lost world. Likewise, Ruth had a duty to
perform; she had to glean in the fields of Boaz. Ruth,
(the Gentile), was sufficed and satisfied, but there
were others who were in need of barley (typical of
Divine truth), for Naomi, who represents the Jew,
and those of the city populace, who typify the unsaved, were greatly in need of the bread *"from
Heaven."* Therefore, Ruth left her Master's presence
to glean in the fields that were waiting for the reapers. How many, as Ruth, have enjoyed seasons of
Divine fellowship and grace. They have desired to
remain at the camp-meetings and prayer services in
fellowship with God's people, but duty called them
elsewhere, to the shops, farms, or places of business,
to work for a livelihood and to bring the truth of the
Gospel of salvation to others through their lives.
There are lost souls that must be saved, wandering
sheep that must be found, discouraged children that
need help. We, like Ruth, must arise and go forward
into the field today. May we learn this lesson well
from the life of Ruth. Let us notice in this study—

> I. **A GRACIOUS PRIVILEGE.**
> II. **A GOODLY PORTION.**
> III. **A GLORIOUS PROSPECT.**

I. A GRACIOUS PRIVILEGE.

If we have duties to perform, the Lord will go before us, as Boaz went before Ruth, and pave the way,
make the hard places easy, and give special instructions to others for our benefit. This reminds us of the
words of the song writer: *"He always takes the heavy
end and gives the light to me."* Often the more diffi-

cult the duty is to perform, the greater is the blessing bestowed and the reward given. Note the threefold privilege—

A. THE DIVINE PRIVILEGE. *"Boaz command-ed."* (v. 15). While she was busy gleaning, Boaz was busy commanding. In the same way, beloved, if we will rise and go into the fields to glean, we shall find that, while we are busy gleaning, our Boaz (Jesus) will be busy commanding. This was a Divine priv-ilege; Boaz gave the permission to glean and instruc-tions to favor the gleaner. Boaz had not forgotten that Ruth had accepted the invitation he gave her— *"At mealtime come thou hither, and eat of the bread, and dip thy morsel in the vinegar."* (v. 14). Her love for Boaz had been expressed in the acceptance of the invitation, but now her love is to be rewarded. He gives special instructions to the young men to allow her to glean among the sheaves and to drop handfuls on purpose for her. He so appreciated her fellowship and communion that now he is going to reward her for the time spent at the table with him. Time spent in communion with Jesus Christ is always rewarded, never wasted. She received more for one-half hour of fellowship and communion with him than she would, had she toiled for days in the field. What a lesson for the believer—in order to have success, time should be spent in fellowship and communion with Him be-fore one goes into the day of gleaning. This is the reason some people seemingly have so many unsuc-cessful days; they neglected their family worship or seasons of secret prayer, depending on their own strength, human ability and intelligence or past ex-periences to help them in their toils for the Master. I have seen the time in my own experience when it seemed that I was so rushed that I could hardly take time to pray, but because of a strong impression by the Holy Spirit, I obeyed the call to prayer. While so engaged, He brought to my mind some important matter which needed immediate attention. Had I rushed on, disregarding the checks of the Spirit to pray, I would have lost far more time. This has been the experience of thousands of others. It would have been so in the case of Ruth. *"Boaz commanded his young men";* this reminds us that it is young men for service and old men for counsel. An older man has gone through the experiences and trials of life and thereby is able to give better counsel than a young man, who is often more active and swifter for service.

B. THE BOUNTIFUL PRIVILEGE. *"Let her glean even among the sheaves."* (v. 15). The sheaves were the large bundles of barley which were set in shocks. Surrounding these shocks of grain there would often be much grain that would be picked up by the reapers in hauling the grain to the thrashing floor. Special permission was given to Ruth to gather this grain for herself. Gleaning was a humble work. It required stooping. In order to be a gleaner in the field of truth and to get the fathoms of God's Word, a person must often stoop in prayer, in humiliation, and in self-abasement. The revelation received in such an attitude is often of the greatest value to a person's life. Revelation given by the Holy Spirit always remains longer in the memory of man than truth received from lip or pen. Gleaning also means toiling. The reason we have so many shallow and un-

learned Christians is because they are not willing to
take time to dig into the Word of Truth to get the
food their souls require. Boaz also commanded saying, *"Let fall also some of the handfuls of purpose for
her, and leave them, that she may glean them."* (v. 16).
Usually gleaning is a slow process; we gather one
spike of grain at a time, but occasionally, as Ruth, we
receive a handful on purpose. Often when the week
has been one of testing and trials, the saint of God goes
to the house of worship with a depressed spirit. Under the inspiration of the Holy Spirit, the preacher
gives just that which the soul needs; the spirit of the
weary one is refreshed because she received a handful
on purpose for her troubled soul through the ministry
of the Holy Spirit, Who understands our needs. Just
when our faith has been stretched to the limit and
trials have gone nearly beyond the mark of endurance,
God drops a big handful on purpose just to lift us to
higher ground. After Peter had denied the Lord and
lied and cursed to the damsel, a special message was
sent to him: *"Go your way, tell his disciples and Peter
that he goeth before you into Galilee."* (Mark 16:7).
This special invitation to backslidden **Peter** was a
handful **(of restoration)** on purpose. Likewise, Paul,
when he was buffeted by the messenger of Satan, *"a
thorn in the flesh,"* received a handful on purpose.
(II Cor. 12:7). He entreated the Lord on three occasions for deliverance from this humiliating condition, but instead of having the thorn removed, he received a handful **(of recognition)** on purpose when the
Lord spoke to him saying, *"My grace is sufficient for
thee: for my strength is made perfect in weakness."*
(II Cor. 12:9). How many of God's dear children have

had handfuls on purpose given them just in the time
of need. While John, the apostle, was a prisoner for
the Word of the Lord on the Isle of Patmos, he was
banished from home, Christian fellowship, and everything that was dear, from an earthly standpoint.
Nevertheless, Christ does not forget His own in an
hour like that, and out of that trying time he received
the wonderful Book of Revelation, which has been
handed down throughout the church age that we
might know what conditions would exist and what
things would transpire up to the closing time of this
dispensation. God knew how to encourage John in the
hour of great need and visited him at this time with
handfuls **(of revelation)** on purpose. In like manner,
God has revealed many precious things to His children while they were passing through trying times
and circumstances.

There are three reasons why Boaz showed this special privilege: **First,** it was because of his love for her.
This is seen in the eighth verse of this chapter where
he bids her *"go not to glean in another field."* This instruction Ruth repeats to her mother-in-law in verse
21: *"He said unto me also, Thou shalt keep fast by
my young men, until they have ended all my harvest."*
Here the love of Boaz for Ruth may be discerned between the lines, for at the closing of the harvest, he
hoped to be the bridegroom in marriage. **Second,** he
extended to her the special privilege because of their
relationship. He knew that he, the kinsman redeemer,
was of near kin to her and expressed it by the term
so often used, *"My daughter."* How the dear Lord al-
lows us to glean among the sheaves and gives us

handfuls on purpose because we are His sons and daughters. How we ought to bless His name for sonship in this Divine family. **Third,** he gave her this privilege because he desired to reward her for the time she spent with him in fellowship and communion, as previously stated in this study. I am sure because of this threefold fact that Jesus (Our Heavenly Boaz) will be sure that we are privileged to glean among the sheaves and will give us handfuls on purpose. We have noticed the Divine Privilege and the Bountiful Privilege. Let us now note—

C. THE UNHINDERED PRIVILEGE. *"Reproach her not."* (v. 15). Boaz wanted her to have liberty as the sheep, which go in and out and find pasture. Jesus said, *"I am the door: by me if any man enter in, he shall be saved, and shall go in and out, and find pasture."* (John 10:9). As the field of Boaz was open to Ruth so the Word of God is open to one and all. The lower we stoop, and the harder we toil, the more God will give to us out of His precious Word. Sacred truth is not received by reading novels and stories that contain no spiritual soul food. Many study the fashion page while their souls are starving for want of food; some listen to worthless entertainment over the radio while the Bible is neglected. Billy Sunday said, *"Show me the books you read, and I will tell you the kind of a person you are."* There are times when the Bible sems to be a dry book, and very little information and spiritual good is obtained from it, but at some future time a person may read the same chapter or portion and receive unmeasured truth from its sacred contents. The difference in the two

occasions is that in the latter reading God's Spirit
was active in revelation. He doesn't want us to be
hindered and desires us to know more and more of
Him, Who is the lily of the valley, the fairest of ten
thousand to the soul.

II. A GOODLY PORTION.

What was Ruth's portion for her day's work? In
verse 17 it says, *"It was about on ephah of barley."*
In a careful study of Exodus 16, we find that the individual amount of manna that the children of Israel
were to gather for their day's supply was *"an omer
for every man."* (v. 16). On the sixth day, they were
to gather twice the amount or *"two omers for one
man."* (v. 22). Peter writes that one day is with the
Lord as one thousand years and one thousand years
as one day. There are to be seven days (one week) of
one thousand years each in the world's history. This
will close the probationary period of the human race,
which may be divided approximately as follows: two
thousand years from creation to Abraham; two thousand years from Abraham to Christ; two thousand
years from Christ to the beginning of the millennial
age; and the seventh day, or the last one thousand
years, is the millennial period, Christ's reign on
earth. This same truth is taught in the first seven
characters in Genesis 5 if the meaning of these
names are studied from a dispensational standpoint.

(1) **Adam and Seth.** The word "Adam" means a
"man of the earth." This reminds us of creation when
man was created by the hand of God. It also reminds
us of the fall of man when sin entered the garden, de-

stroying their righteousness and holiness and passing
upon them the sentence of death, which was given by
God because of their act of disobedience. The name
"Seth" means *"appointed or put."* (Gen. 4:25, margin). This reminds us of Abraham, who after the
first two thousand years was about to offer up his son
Isaac on Mount Moriah. It was there that God **put**
the ram in the thicket and appointed him to die in
the place of Isaac. (Gen. 22:13). This was prophetic
of the death of Christ, Who was appointed by God to
die in the place of fallen man.

(2) **Enos and Cainan.** These two men covered the
two thousand year period (representatively) from
Abraham to the time of Christ. The word *"Enos"*
means *"mortality or death."* This reminds us of the
law that was given to the children of Israel on Mount
Sinai in the third thousand years of the world's history; the penalty for the broken law was death. The
word *"Cainan"* means *"to purchase."* This brings us
up to the birth of Christ, which occurred in the last
part of the fourth thousand years. He came to purchase the lost estate and buy back that which man
lost through the fall. Thus, we are bought with a
price, and that price is the blood of Christ.

(3) **Mahalaleel and Jared.** Mahalaleel means *"praise
of God."* This brings us into the fifth thousand years,
the beginning of the dispensation of grace when the
church of the first-born was the *"praise of God."* The
named *"Jared"* means "descending." The closing of
the sixth thousand years will be in terrific judgment
when the wrath of God shall descend from Heaven

on the God defiers and Christ-rejecters on the earth. This period will be known as the great tribulation which will close with descending judgment which is now incomprehensible.

(4) **Enoch.** This means *"a teacher or one who imparts knowledge."* This portrays the millennial age when His righteousness shall cover the earth and all shall know the Lord from the least of them to the greatest of them. (Jer. 31:34). This seventh thousand years cannot occur until after the Church of the living God has been raptured to Heaven and the tribulation has passed. This is typified in this character we are now discussing, Enoch, the seventh from Adam, *"who was not for God took him."* (Gen. 5:24). The Israelites on the sixth day had to gather two omers, which was to be enough for the sixth and seventh days, typical of the church age and the millennial age. If we would reign with Christ in the coming dispensation, it is now time to gather manna. As the seventh day closes up the week, we have a new beginning in the eighth day, which will be the beginning of a new creation. This will be the ages of ages so beautifully portrayed in Revelation, chapters 21 and 22. In the closing verses of Exodus 16, it tells the amount of an omer, *"Now an omer is the tenth part of an ephah."* (Exodus 16:36). If Ruth gathered an ephah, she gathered ten times the amount of one omer, (an Israelite's portion for one day) or a ten days' supply. If barley typifies Christ in incarnation, crucifixion, and resurrection, as described in the previous chapter, she had sufficient to supply her from the ascension of Christ to the descent of the Holy Spirit, which was a period of ten

days. How beautifully the whole scheme of redemption is pictured in this little Book of Ruth.

THE NUMBER TEN

Ten in the Scripture is the number of responsibility. God gives us ten toes to walk with and ten fingers to work with; the Israelites had ten commandments, for the keeping of which they were responsible. There were ten spies responsible for the report brought back from Canaan's land. The ten virgins were responsible for their spiritual condition when going out to meet the bridegroom. Again, tithes, or one part out of ten, were demanded by God from Israel, being the measure of their responsibility in giving. Likewise, God held Naomi and Elimelech responsible for their ten years of wandering in the land of Moab. (Ruth 1:4). There were ten elders of the city who sat at the gate as responsible witnesses to the transaction accomplished by Boaz in redeeming the lost estate and becoming the bridegroom of Ruth. (Ruth 4:2). There were ten generations mentioned in the closing verses of this Book, who were responsible in bringing forth David, who is typical of the Redeemer, Jesus Christ. We find there are no errors or mistakes in God's Word concerning dates, numbers, types, and dispensations. It all dovetails together, making a complete and perfect plan.

Note the three splendid qualifications Ruth possessed:

    A. HER FAITHFULNESS.

    B. HER CAREFULNESS.

    C. HER THOUGHTFULNESS.

A. HER FAITHFULNESS. *"She gleaned in the field until even."* (v. 17). She was not like those who begin in the evening of their lives and have nothing to present to God but the ashes of an idle and misspent life; she started her gleaning in the morning and continued until evening. All the bright and sunny portion of her life, she spent in the Master's service. How it behooves the young people to seek Him in their youth, while He may be found, that they may spend their days in service and sacrifice in the Master's kingdom, that they may, at the close of life's day, have a good supply and a great reward for their toils of life. Gleaning sometimes is slow work, but if we save what we gather, it will increase, yes, even multiply, and at the close of the day, we will not come empty handed into Boaz's (Christ's) presence. There is no place for a lazy Christian in God's kingdom. Dr. Watson once said, "Many talk about the upper room but live in the basement." Those in the upper room were engaged in supplication and prayer and, no doubt, were reviewing the words of the Master. The Christian's life should be a busy life, busy in communion and in study of His Word, busy in winning souls and encouraging others. You will find that the person who is thus engaged is always the greatest blessing.

B. HER CAREFULNESS. She *"beat out that she had gleaned."* (v. 17). It is not only our duty to be faithful in gleaning but also to be careful to beat out the chaff from the grain we have gleaned. The beating out process is too often neglected by some people. Some sermons need thrashing, for it is certain that there is a portion of straw and chaff in some of them. Not everything that is preached is Scriptural, nor is everything light to the listener, but some people after hearing a message, thrash the preacher with their tongues rather than the sermon with their gospel flails. There may be a lot of straw and chaff— quantity but no quality. Ruth wanted the bulky chaff removed that she might have pure grain to carry home. If people would search the Word in analyzing the sermon, it would spare many the danger and the sorrow of falling into error. What we need today is Berean Christians, for they *"were more noble than those in Thessalonica, in that they received the word with all readiness of mind, and searched the scriptures daily, whether those things were so."* (Acts 17:11). It is not the Word of God that forms the chaff, but it is the misinterpretation. Let the chaff go to the wind and the straw to the fire, but retain the wheat, the solid grain of truth, within your own heart and mind, that you may be able to hand it on to others after you have been sufficed. One has said: "Preach the word: if you can't eat the chaff yourself, don't give it to another."

C. HER THOUGHTFULNESS. *"S h e brought forth, and gave to her* (mother-in-law) *that she had reserved after she was sufficed."* (v. 18). After Ruth was rewarded for her day of toil, she *"went into the city."* (v. 18). This pictures a place of need. God will not give us special privileges to glean among the sheaves and receive handfuls on purpose to hoard for ourselves, He gives it to us that we may go to the populace and distribute to those in need. Jesus said, *"Give, and it shall be given."* Communion through

the Word and fellowship in prayer are seen in the
two acts—gleaning and beating. To be just a student
of the Word without a life of prayer makes one a
formalist. There will be truth but no glory; facts but
no fire. To spend much time in prayer but to neglect the study of the Word will cause one to become
a fanatic. Prayer and study must go hand in hand.
Prayer puts power and force back of the truth, thus
causing it to have an effect upon the needy living in
the regions of the city. For that reason I seldom go
to prayer without taking my Bible that I might feed
my prayer on the promises of God and at the same
time receive revelations of truth for my soul.

Some writers have criticized Ruth by saying that
she looked after her own personal interest first before
passing on the grain to Naomi, but if we look at it
from a spiritual standpoint, this is not so. She could
not give to Naomi until she had first been satisfied
herself. Her own soul had to be fed before she could
feed others. *"Faith must feed on its gathered store
before it can impart to others."* (S. Ridout). Here is
also dispensational truth. Naomi, who is a type of
the Jew, could receive no blessing or sacred spiritual
truth unless it came through Ruth, a type of the
Church. The Jew of today can receive no spiritual
help unless it comes through the Church. The Holy
Spirit, the indweller and the abider in the body of
Christ, must convict them, in the same way as He
does the Gentiles, through the Word of God to con-
vince them of their error and their sin. May the
Church of Jesus Christ see from this their responsibility in passing on the truth of the Gospel to the Jew,

which is typified by Naomi. Ruth expressed the true
spirit of Christianity when she shared with others
that which she had received from the hand of Boaz,
but how slow Christianity is today in giving the Gospel to the multiplied heathen who have never yet
enjoyed one grain of spiritual barley (incarnation,
crucifixion, and resurrection of Christ). They are
dying without ever having any knowledge of gospel
light.   May the reader ponder over the following
words of my gospel song entitled, "Dying Without
Gospel Light":

While we humbly kneel and pray,
Heathen living far away
Grope in darkness void of grace,
Hurrying on with rapid pace.

While we worship at His feet,
Countless millions must repeat,
"We have never heard of Him
Who can save the soul from sin."

While our fellowship is sweet,
Heathen by the score you'll meet
In the regions of distress,
Never have such happiness.

While we're nearing Heaven's door,
Heathen dying by the score
Close their eyes in darkest night,
Dying without gospel light.

While we're singing round the throne,
Safely we are gathered Home,
Millions barred outside the gate
For the Gospel once did wait.

III. A GLORIOUS PROSPECT.

Ruth had secured a good supply and returned with

the barley to her mother-in-law. Naomi *"saw what she had gleaned."* (v. 18). If we have been faithful, careful, and thoughtful, as the previous side-headings indicate, others will see it by the amount of spiritual truth we can produce. It is impossible to hide our light under a bushel. Others will readily see that we have been gleaning and then beating out that which we have gleaned. In other words, a life of communion through the Word and a life of fellowship in prayer cannot be hid. In the introduction of this book, I mentioned that the Book could be studied—

First, HISTORICALLY.

Second, DISPENSATIONALLY.

Third, EXPERIMENTALLY.

This truth can be plainly seen in these last few verses we are now reviewing in this chapter. I will call your attention to them as we reach the verses. There are three words beginning with "K," which I would like to use as subdivisions under this heading, namely— knowledge, kindness, and kinsman.

A. THE KNOWLEDGE. (v. 19). Naomi asks Ruth, *"Where hast thou gleaned today? and where wroughtest thou?"* (v. 19). She saw the splendid supply Ruth had obtained for her day's toil, but now God is going to reveal to Naomi something far greater than the knowledge of the field where Ruth had toiled. She is now to know the owner of the field, Boaz. Naomi at once pronounces a blessing upon Boaz by saying, *"Blessed be he that did take knowledge of thee."* (v. 19). While bestowing this blessing, she

was unconscious of the fact that the blessing was upon
Boaz, the near kinsman. Here is a dispensational
truth. She was still in the dark as the Jews are today. The Jews realize that blessings are being bestowed upon them, but they are unaware that these
blessings come directly through Jesus Christ, their
own kinsman, according to the seed of David. Likewise, Naomi was unaware that it was Boaz, the near
kinsman, that was bestowing upon them these special
favors and blessings in giving them handfuls on purpose. Then Ruth slowly unfolds the truth by saying,
*"The man's name with whom I wrought today is
Boaz."* (v. 19). Here Naomi is given firsthand information as to who the bestower of the blessing was.
I wonder if we Gentiles are giving the Jews the information of which they stand in need—that the untold blessings they are receiving in these last days
are from the hand of their Kinsman Redeemer, Who
was of the seed of David, of the tribe of Judah, Who
was born in Bethlehem, and Who is the Bread of Life
for the world. The word **"knowledge"** is from the
Hebrew word *"nakar,"* which means *"to discern or
make a distinction."* The word is twice translated
"knowledge" in the Old Testament; they are both in
this chapter, verses 10 and 19. It emphasizes that
Boaz had made a distinction in Ruth. How wonderfully that points forward to the dispensation of grace
when God through Jesus Christ made a distinction
in the Gentiles, who were without God and without
hope in the world. How we ought to unite with
Naomi and say, *"Blessed be he that did take knowledge of us."*

B. THE KINDNESS. (v. 20). Naomi had been

informed that the owner of the field, who gave the handfuls on purpose, was Boaz. She said, *"Blessed be he of the Lord, who hath not left off his kindness to the living and to the dead."* That her eyes were fully opened can be seen by the manner of her blessing. In the previous verses she said, *"Blessed be he,"* but in this blessing she adds a few words and says, *"Blessed be he of the Lord."* She realized that God's hand was in it all. The new convert blesses Jesus Christ in the same manner today. He realizes His divinity and expresses it by saying, *"Blessed be he of the Lord."* Slowly the scales had dropped from the eyes of Naomi; so it will be with the Jewish remnant in the last days. In this blessing (*"who hath not left off his kindness to the living and to the dead"*) we can see the threefold teaching of the Book, **historically, dispensationally,** and **experimentally.**

First, Historically. Naomi had been living in Moab so long that she had forgotten her kindred in the land of Israel until God, by a slow process of revelation, revealed them to her. She is reminded that Boaz had showed kindness to the dead, that is to Elimelech and the two sons. The kindness extended to her husband in former days is not stated, but for some reason Boaz is showing the same spirit of kindness to the living now (Naomi and Ruth) that he did in former days to Elimelech and his sons.

Second, Dispensationally. The living is here typified by Ruth, the Gentile, while the dead represents the Jewish people. As a nation, the Jews are dead and buried in the graveyard of nations according to the teaching of Ezekiel, chapter 37, where it tells how the prophet was shown a valley of dry bones and was asked the question, *"Son of man, can these bones live?"* (v. 3). Many of the readers know the story how Ezekiel prophesied to these bones, commanding them to hear the word of the Lord, and how a promise was given him that breath would re-enter; sinews, flesh, and skin would appear upon the bones; and they would live. While he was prophesying the miracle occurred, and they stood upon their feet. The number of people was so large that it constituted a great army. The Lord said unto Ezekiel this army of people *"are the whole house of Israel."* (v. 11). *"And ye shall know that I am the Lord, when I have opened your graves, O my people, and brought you up out of your graves, And shall put my spirit in you, and ye shall live."* (v's. 13, 14). Thus by a careful study of this chapter, it can be seen that Judah (the two tribes) and Israel (the ten tribes) will be raised up in national resurrection and united together as portrayed by the two sticks, which were joined together in the hand of the prophet. It will do the reader good to take time to study this chapter. The Jews are now passing through a state of death, but the springtime is coming, the fig tree is budding, and we know that summer is nigh, that life for the dead is close at hand. In the meantime, while the Jewish nation has been lying in a state of death, God has been extending His kindness to the living, the Gentile people, represented by Ruth.

Third, Experimentally. In the preceding thought we have studied Israel as a nation, but we will now consider these verses from the standpoint of Church truth. In the Book of Ephesians, the second chapter, Paul writes *"You hath he quickened, who were dead in trespasses and sins."* The word *"you"* refers to those who are now alive in Christ. They have been quickened and raised from the state of spiritual death. The same power that raised Jesus from the dead is now able to raise men out of degradation and sin, and by the kindness of God the Father (v. 7) through Jesus Christ, the *"you"* of the text have been made alive by *"his workmanship, created in Christ Jesus."* (v. 10). Thus, the Christian of the present day is not a reformed man, but he is a transformed or a new created man, having new life, new desires, and new ambitions; old things have passed away and all things have become new. May I emphasize that Christianity is not church membership, reformation, new resolutions, or good parentage, but it is life in Christ Jesus— life imparted into the soul that gives man a new walk, new hopes, and new aspirations. But to whom does the word *"ye"* in verse two refer? *"Wherein in time past ye walked according to the course of this world."* The **"ye"** of the text were the Gentiles who were living in a state of death because of trespasses and sins, who were under the dominion of the Prince of the power of the air. Paul continues in the following verse by saying, *"Among whom also we all had our conversation in times past in the lusts of our flesh."* There we have the Jew included in the term **"we,"** for Paul was an Israelite of the tribe of Benjamin, a Hebrew of the Hebrews. The Church of Jesus Christ is composed of those called out from among the Jews and Gentiles, those who were dead in trespasses and sins but who are made alive through the resurrection of Jesus Christ. The object and purpose of it all is shown in the seventh verse of the chapter we are discussing, *"That in the ages to come he might shew the exceeding riches of his grace in his kindness toward us through Christ Jesus."* In this chapter we find the term **"ye,"** representing the Gentiles; **"we,"** representing the Jews; and **"us,"** representing the Church composed of Jew and Gentile. These will be put on display in the ages to come that the exceeding riches of His grace in His **kindness** may be manifested throughout all eternity. Certainly here is a shouting point. May all the people say "Amen," rejoice, and bring glory to His name.

The thought we have been studying is the **kindness** that He has shown to the living and to the dead. Here we have it pictured in His **kindness** toward us through Jesus Christ by giving us the exceeding riches of His grace in His redemption, in raising us out of the graveyard of sin that **in the ages to come** He may exhibit us before Satan, a fallen world, and unholy men, the trophies of His marvelous work of redemption, wrought by the sacrifice and resurrection of His own Son. The object of all this was not for time, but for eternity, **"in the ages to come."** After Satan has been cast into the lake of fire, after sin has been annihilated, after time is replaced by eternity, after sorrow and tears are wiped away, after death has died to rise no more, after man has ceased gaining his livelihood by the sweat of his brow, after the curse on a wrecked creation has been completely lifted, these redeemed ones shall dwell with Him forever and ever, "the ages to come." What **kindness** He is extending to the

living, the Gentiles, and to the dead, the Jews. Thus
we can plainly see in this verse the historical, dispensational, and experimental teaching of this book.

C. THE KINSMAN. (v. 20). Naomi says to
Ruth, *"The man is near of kin unto us."* (The margin
reads: *"One that hath right to redeem."*) By this
statement Naomi acknowledges the kinsman. The relationship that exists has dawned upon her, and dispensationally, in the same process of revelation
(which has been rather slow) the Jews will be made
to see that Jesus Christ, Whom their ancestors forced
to the cross, was the Messiah. It was in this slow manner that Christ revealed Himself to the Samaritan
woman as recorded in the fourth chapter of John. Jesus, tired and weary, sat on the well. He Who had
created all, even the water within the well, now
stoops in humiliation and begs a drink from the
Samaritan woman. *"Give me to drink."* (v. 7). The
woman replies, *"How is it that thou, being a Jew,
askest drink of me, which am a woman of Samaria?"*
(v. 9). She saw Jesus at this time as just a weary,
thirsty **Jew.** Slowly He unfolded to her His Messiah-
ship by telling her of the water He had to give, living water, and that if she would drink of this water,
she would never thirst again. When she acknowledged that Jacob's well was deep, it was a hint of a
weary existence, and that it was through toil and
labor that she came at the noonday hour, in the heat
of the day, and drew water from this well. It was
customary for women to carry the water in the
morning and in the evening, but sin had ostracized
her from the companionship of the feminine society

of her day. The woman expresses her desire to
have this water that she may be relieved of the task
and hardship that was placed upon her. In reply to
this request, Jesus said, *"Go, call thy husband, and
come hither."* (v. 16). The woman answered, *"I have
no husband."* She was trying to cover up her sin by
truth when she made that answer. Jesus reminded her
that she had five husbands but now was living with a
man that was not her husband. Here the revelation of
Christ goes a little deeper, and she confesses, *"I per-
ceive that thou art a prophet."* (v. 19). He is no longer a weary Jew in her sight, but now He is a **Prophet**
of the Lord. At once their conversation drifts into the
thought of worship. The woman expresses her hope
in a coming Messiah and even goes so far as to give
His name (Christ) and His work (He will tell us all
things). Then Jesus brings to her the third revelation
by saying, *"I that speak unto thee am he."* (v. 26).
Immediately she left her water pots (the symbol of
her sinful toil), went into the city, and spoke to the
men (probably those with whom she had lived) saying, *"Come, see a man, which told me all things that
ever I did: is not this the Christ?"* (v. 29). Now she
acknowledges Him as the Messiah, the Son of God.
How beautifully this chapter shows the slow process
of revelation: First, a **Jew;** second, a **Prophet;** third,
the **Messiah.** May we take a lesson from this and not
be too hasty in condemning those who may not see
the light as rapidly as we think they should. I wish to
add that there are two persons to whom the Lord re-
veals the true character of Himself: To the **outcast
sinner,** which we have just reviewed in the case of the
Samaritan woman, and to the **outcast saint,** the blind

young man in John 9:35-38, He revealed Himself as
the Messiah, the Son of God.

We will not give the duty of the kinsman redeemer
under this division but will explain that later in the
study of the book. However, if we read carefully and
prayerfully between the lines, we can see one hint
given here in the statement of Ruth to Naomi when
she said, *"He said unto me also, Thou shalt keep fast
by my young men, until they have ended all my harvest."* (v. 21). Let us notice the *"also"* of this quotation. Boaz had instructed her to keep fast by the
young men until they had ended all the harvest. Here
is a prediction that at the close of the harvest Boaz
would accomplish one of the duties of the kinsman—
that was to marry the wife of the deceased relative.
Here is a blessed thought for those to whom He has
extended kindness; that is when the *"harvest is past,
the summer is ended,"* (Jer. 8:20), the Bridegroom
Kinsman and the bride of Christ will be united in
marriage. Naomi (typical of the Jewish remnant)
now takes on new faith, which is evident by her instruction to Ruth when she says, *"It is good, my
daughter, that thou go out with his maidens, that they
meet thee not in any other field."* (v. 22). What a
warning it should be to the Gentile believer today, especially at the close of this dispensation, when the
harvest is almost past, that they find "thee not in any
other field." What sorrow and distress will befall the
man that is found in the field of the world when the
Heavenly Boaz comes to take His bride to the bridal
chambers in the sky. It will be for your eternal good
to follow the example of Ruth, for *"she kept fast by
the maidens of Boaz to glean unto the end of the*

barley harvest and of wheat harvest." (v. 23). We are closing this chapter, leaving Ruth dwelling with her mother-in-law at the close of the harvest. Just a word in closing: the grace of Jesus Christ is so wonderful that the Gentile and the Jew, represented by Ruth and her mother-in-law, can live harmoniously together, embracing the same faith, worshiping the same Christ, bowing at the same altar, enjoying the same hope, having intercession by the same High Priest, feeding on the same truth, and communing in the same spirit. It is the grace of God that can make enemies, friends, yea, brethren in Christ, and cause them to live in the realms of love and unity. This same truth can be applied to domestic realms where grace can be supplied to live with a much abused person, such as the "*mother-in-law.*"

THE DEVOTION AND THE REWARD

STUDY SIX

(Ruth 3:1-18)

In our last study we saw Ruth gleaning with the maidens until the close of the barley and wheat harvests. The first thought of this study is Naomi seeking rest for her daughter-in-law, Ruth. This brings us to the second division of the Book. Our first five studies covered the first division of the Book; the key thought was "FIND GRACE." These last two chapters, which we are about to consider, gives us the second division of the Book, the main thought being "FIND REST."

In a previous study, I explained the seven feasts of the Lord found in Leviticus 23. **First,** was the feast of the Passover, pointing forward to the Lamb of God, Who would die upon the cross. **Second,** there was the feast of unleavened bread, which speaks of fellowship in a separated walk with Jesus Christ. **Third,** was the feast of first-fruits, giving the thought of resurrection of Christ. The Israelites took a handful of barley grain and waved it before the Lord. This was waved up and down and in and out in the form of a cross, speaking of Christ's triumphant resurrection from the death of the cross. **Fourth,** came the feast of Pentecost, the time of the wheat harvest, which followed about fifty days after the barley harvest. The barley harvest prefigured the first installment of grace, which spoke of new life on the grounds of resurrection, but fifty days later at the feast of Pentecost they were to receive the second installment of Divine grace by the baptism of the Holy Spirit. This was represented by the wheat harvest.

In the 147th Psalm we find a prophetic picture. David is exhorting Zion to *"Praise thy God."* (v's. 12-14). Here we have a large pod with four "P's" in it: Praise Him — (1) for His **Power,** *"For he hath strengthened the bars of thy gates";* (2) for His **Providence,** *"He hath blessed thy children within thee";* (3) for His **Peace,** *"He maketh peace in thy borders";* (4) for His **Provision,** *"Filleth thee with the finest of the wheat."* You will note that the Psalmist says, *"The finest of the wheat."* The term *"finest"* is from the Hebrew word, *"cheleb,"* which means *"the fat"* or the best part of the wheat. Israel raised barley, rye, and wheat, but the finest of these three grains was wheat, which was typical of Pentecost. You will notice that at the close of this wheat harvest Naomi is seeking *"rest"* for Ruth. The word *"rest"* is the same Hebrew word found in Psalm 95:11, where God swore in His wrath *"that they should not enter into my rest."* The **rest** here spoken of was Canaan's **rest.** What Canaan's land was to Israel a consecrated, Spirit-filled life is to the New Testament believer. A life of victory over our enemies, a life of provision for our souls, a life of power for service, and a life of freedom from sin—such is the higher life provided for the believer in the baptism of the Spirit.

Israel accepted the report of the eight spies and refused to enter the land of Canaan. This brought forth the wrath of God, and for forty years Israel wandered in the wilderness. God said in His wrath that they should not possess the land of Canaan because of their unbelief. The truth in this Psalm (95:11) is brought forth by the writer to the Hebrews, chapters three and four. He warns the brethren to take heed lest there be in them *"an evil heart of unbelief in departing from the living God."* (Heb. 3:12). He urges the believers to *"exhort one another daily, while it is called To-day,"* and warns them that they are in danger of forfeiting their position in grace by failing to enter into the rest provided for the *"people of God."* (Chapter 4:9). He also warns them in verse one by saying, *"Let us therefore fear, lest, a promise being left us of entering into his rest, any of you should seem to come short of it."* The reader will do well to study these two chapters and to see that the call to the second rest is *"To-day."* The word *"To-day"* is found five times in these two chapters, showing the importance of seeking and obtaining this rest now, not at some future time. From this we can plainly see that the teaching of the Book of Ruth is—first, to **"find grace,"** yes, grace to cover all our sin; second, to **"find rest"**—an experimental soul-rest for the child of God.

This teaching is also found in the words of Jesus, *"Come unto me, all ye that labour and are heavy laden, and I will give you rest."* There we find rest for the laborer, the man who would gain Heaven by good works; rest for the heavy laden, the man who is crushed in spirit because of his sinful life and who carries a load of sin on his heart. Jesus said, *"Come* (not go) .. *and I will give you rest."* Jesus continues to speak to those now who have found this first rest by saying, *"Take my yoke upon you, and learn of me; for I am meek and lowly in heart: and ye shall find rest unto your souls.*" (Matt. 11:29). The sinner is nowhere urged to take the yoke upon him and start working in His vineyard. That is a call to the believer. The sinner is not urged to learn of Him but to seek Him, for he cannot learn of Him until first he has found Him. The result is that the believer will *"Find Rest"* for his soul. This is the second rest. First, he is given rest from his sins as Israel was given rest from a life of bondage in Egypt, but second, he is to *"Find Rest"* as Israel found it in the land of Canaan. The burden of our next two chapters is *"Find Rest."* Naomi desired to *"Find Rest"* for Ruth that it might be well with her. (Ruth 3:1). The three main divisions of this study are:

I.   **PERSONAL OBEDIENCE.**
II. **PLACE OF OBTAINMENT.**
III. **PENTECOSTAL OUTCOME.**

I.   PERSONAL OBEDIENCE.

(Chap. 3:1-5). *"All that thou sayest unto me I will do."* (v. 5). It is the good and obedient that will eat the fat of the land. The Holy Ghost is given to those who obey Him. (Acts 5:32). The reason Paul received an inheritance among them that are sanctified was because he was not *"disobedient unto the heavenly vision."* (Acts 26:19). The sanctifying grace of the Spirit can never come into the heart of the believer who is not entirely consecrated and fully obedient in every respect. The three divisions under this main division, "PERSONAL OBEDIENCE," are—

A. THE PERSONAL RELATIONSHIP.
B. THE PREPARATION REQUIRED.
C. THE PLACE REFERRED.

A.   THE PERSONAL RELATIONSHIP. *"And now is not Boaz of our kindred, with whose maidens thou wast?"* (v. 2). Boaz and Ruth are both identified in this verse; Boaz is revealed as the kindred redeemer. The personal relationship is here explained. Before we can have the rest God has provided for us in redemption, there must be a personal relationship. We must be born into His family and be called *"sons and daughters of the Lord Almighty."* Ruth is identified by the words *"with whose maidens thou wast."* It classes her with the gleaners of the harvest, and we can also read in these words her obedience to the command of Boaz—*"Go not to glean in another field, but abide here fast by my maidens."* (Chap. 2:8, 22). Because of her perfect obedience to him, she is now qualified as a candidate to obtain the rest that Boaz could provide and to be later united in marriage to him. Had she not obeyed him, it would have been otherwise.

I wish you to note—

The harvest is now past. The reaping of the barley and wheat has been completed, and it has been brought to the threshing floor. There is but little gleaning left to be done. The barley and wheat have been gathered. A beautiful dispensational picture is here taught. It shows that it is the closing period of this age, and as we are nearing the last part of the Book, the dispensational fullness is becoming more complete—the wedding is not far hence. The summer has ended, the harvest is past, and at the close of this age in which we are now living, it seems that all that can be done is a little gleaning here and there. The days of great revivals are past; multitudes will not flock to the Lord

for salvation. Nearly every fundamental pastor of today will tell you that it is much harder to bring men
into the fold of Christ now than it was fifteen years
ago. It is contradictory to Scripture to teach that there
will be a world-wide revival in the last days, for the
Word of God teaches, *"That in the last days perilous
times shall come. For men shall be lovers of their own
selves . . . from such turn away."* (II Tim. 3:1-5).
The Spirit of God said: *"In the latter times* (last
days) *some shall depart from the faith, giving heed to
seducing spirits, and doctrines of devils."* (I Tim. 4:-
1). Paul warns Timothy that evil men and seducers
shall wax worse and worse, deceiving and being deceived. (II Tim. 3:13). In the parable of the great
supper (Luke 14:15-24), Jesus taught that the last
guests that are brought to the Marriage Supper of the
Lamb would have to be brought in by force—*"Compel
them to come in."* (v. 23). The word *"compel"* is
from the Greek word *"necessitate,"* meaning *"to con-
strain, to compel by force."* John the Revelator plainly described the Laodicean period (Chap. 3:14-22), in
which even the professing Church of the last days
will bar Christ from its presence, and He will be
standing, knocking at the door, pleading for admit-
tance.

Christ also said, *"When the Son of man cometh,
shall he find faith on the earth?"* (Luke 18:8). By this,
we know that at Christ's second coming there will be
scarcely any faith on the earth. In James 5:1-12 he
describes a condition that will exist between the rich
and the poor in the *"last days."* He shows how the
laborers who have performed the work for the rich

men will be defrauded of the portion which rightly belongs to them. The laborers' cries (because of their poverty and need) will reach the ears of Jehovah, and the gold and silver which the rich men have defrauded from them will become a witness against them while accumulated wealth will be as fire in their bosoms. This prophecy is actually being fulfilled today. Scores of rich men have lost their vast estates, and some have entered bankruptcy. The gold in which they trusted has been confiscated by the government; the real estate which has been the pride of many has lost its value, and the taxes upon it have increased to such an extent that many have been unable to pay them. Stocks and bonds in which people have trusted are valued today as a scrap of paper. In some countries the rich man's property and finances have been confiscated, and he is left in the role of the beggar. In this chapter, (James 5:1-12), the brethren (the followers of Christ) are urged to be patient and to establish their hearts because "the coming of the Lord draweth nigh." (v. 8). They are warned not to complain against each other because some may enjoy more prosperity than they. James tells that that would lead to condemnation. (v. 9). He then points to Job as an example of patience. It was he that saw *"the end of the Lord,"* (v. 11), meaning Job saw how the Lord would deal in the end when He restored to him the confidence and friendship of his false comforters and gave him *"twice as much as he had before."* He was comforted in spite of all evil that had come upon him and in the latter end he had more than in the beginning. (Job 42:7-17). From the many Scriptures which we

have just quoted, it is surely evident that there will
be no world-wide awakening or revival in the last
days. Such is the dark picture of the last days from
the Word of God.

A further proof of the dark condition of the age is
seen by the fact that the winnowing process is done
in the evening. The day's work has been completed;
the sun is setting in the western horizon of the dispensation of grace; there are but a few hours before
the midnight darkness of the tribulation will be setting in. Political, financial, social, and spiritual storms
are brooding over the evening atmosphere. The reader can plainly see that this time is now upon us. The
political distress can be seen in our state capitals and
in Washington. Men in the same parties are no longer
standing shoulder to shoulder, but they are quarrel-
ing and contending among themselves. The financial
condition is even worse. Many banks have failed;
thousands have closed their doors. The gold in which
men trusted can no longer be called their own, but it
is now in possession of our government. The real estate that men depended on is now highly taxed and
yet has decreased in value as much as 75 per cent.
Men who were worth millions five years ago are now
in bankruptcy. Such is the financial distress of today.
The social condition is no better. The beer gardens,
cigarette-smoking women, the immoral dance halls,
the moving pictures with suggestive teaching, and a
thousand other things too numerous to mention are
all bringing about a social wreckage in our nation.
Yet, while this is true, the true bride of Christ is going to higher heights in Christian grace by seeking

the baptism of the Spirit of God and are living lives of holiness unto the Lord, thus getting their wedding garments ready.

We are in the sifting time of this age. Many who are not willing to take the line of complete separation and identify themselves with a separate, called-out, sanctified bride of Christ shall depart from the faith. It is not midnight nor the dark portion of the night just before daybreak, but it is evening. The sun is setting, spiritual light is diminishing, evangelistic efforts are ceasing, and missionary enterprises are at a low ebb. The threshing time has arrived; the grain with the straw and chaff must be thrown up to the evening wind, which is typical of the Holy Spirit, Who will aid the Church in the last days to prepare itself for the great event just ahead—the rapture of the saints. Thank God for the Holy Ghost, Who is in the world to prepare the bride for the Marriage of the Lamb. It is no wonder that God has raised up so many camp meetings, prophetic Bible conferences, and other coaling stations where the saints of God can receive the teaching of full salvation and be empowered with the Spirit of God that they might live holy and righteous in the last days. I said the sifting time, when the chaff, the straw, and all the valueless material will be separated from the wheat, is at hand. This is the process that the Church is passing through in these last days. Let us note—

B. THE PREPARATION REQUIRED. *"Wash thyself therefore, and anoint thee, and put thy raiment upon thee."* (v. 3). In this preparation, you will see three things: (1) **The need of cleansing.** *"Wash* *thyself."* As Ruth needed cleansing, the unsanctified believer needs purity. *"Christ also loved the church, and gave himself for it; That he might sanctify and cleanse it with the washing of water by the word."* (Eph. 5:25, 26). In the Tabernacle study, the priest brought the sacrifice and made his decision at the gate. He found his acceptance at the altar on the grounds of shed blood, but the cleansing was provided at the laver, which was made of the looking-glasses of the women, typical of the Word of God. James 1:23, 24 refers to this. Every spiritual and moral blemish can be seen as we study the Word of God. However, provisions have been made for the removal of the blemish. The water in the laver, with which the priest could wash, came from the smitten rock. It was typical of the Holy Ghost that descended on Pentecost after the Son of God died on the Cross of Calvary that He might *"sanctify and cleanse it* (the Church) *with the washing of water by the word."* (Eph. 5:26). In this verse you will notice the three "W's" found in connection with the laver: **First,** the Word typified by the brazen looking-glasses; **second,** the Water in the laver, typical of the Holy Spirit; and **third,** the Washing which is the cleansing effected by the baptismal process wrought upon the believer by the Holy Spirit.

(2) **The need of power.** *"Anoint thee."* (Ruth 3:3). The word *"anoint"* is from the Hebrew word *"suk"* meaning *"to pour out."* This foretells how the Holy Spirit was to be poured out on the day of Pentecost, filling and anointing the apostles for service. There is not only the need of cleansing for the believer, but there is the need in these days of the anointing of the

Holy Ghost in the ministry of the Word, prayer, testimony, and personal work. In fact, in every part of church work, men who take an active part should be anointed with power from on high. It was customary for the people of Israel to anoint themselves with oil. Oil was a type of the Holy Spirit as found in the holy anointing oil of the Old Testament, which contained five ingredients. Five is the number of grace. This points forward to this dispensation when the Holy Spirit would anoint the believers in the body of Christ. When Elijah asked Elisha what he should do for him before he took his departure in a chariot of fire, *"Elisha said, I pray thee, let a double portion of thy spirit be upon me."* (II Kings 2:9). It was a noble thing to request not gold, nor silver, nor raiment for himself, but a double portion of the Spirit that he might have it to meet the condition of his day, at which time the apostasy of Ahab was at its height. What is more needed today in the Church of Jesus Christ than the anointing of the Holy Ghost on individuals and collective bodies, as pictured in the double portion of Elisha? In his case, self was completely set aside, and the need of Israel in its apostate condition was foremost in his mind.

(3) **The need of the wedding garment.** *"Put thy raiment upon thee."* Boaz, the kinsman, was near at hand; the wedding day was not far distant; it was high time to make the preparation. In preparing for an earthly matrimonial ceremony, about the last item usually considered is the wedding garment. Likewise, in the case of the marriage of Jesus and His bride, the last work of this dispensation will be the

preparing of the bride for this glorious event. At this time, when the world, as a whole, has practically rejected the salvation of Jesus Christ and the barley and wheat harvests are over, the true saints of God who have heard and believed the message *"Behold, the bridegroom cometh,"* will purify themselves by meeting the conditions laid down in the Word of God and will thus be prepared for the marriage of the Lamb.

C. THE PLACE REFERRED. *"Threshing-floor."* In II Samuel, chapter 24, you will find the story of David numbering Israel and the judgment that came on the nation because their king failed to number them according to God's rule. God had provided a plan, which they were to follow in numbering Israel. Each Israelite over twenty years of age was qualified for war by bringing to the priest one-half shekel of silver, called the atonement money. David in numbering Israel left out the thought of atonement by failing to demand payment of the atonement money. How many preachers today are numbering their congregations outside of the atonement of Jesus Christ, including all those who have never been born again and those who have backslidden, having departed from the way of righteousness. When David was about to number the people, Joab, the captain of the hosts, protested against this manner of numbering Israel, but on the demand of David, Joab went from Dan to Beersheba, numbering all the tribes. He reported that there were eight hundred thousand men in Israel and five hundred thousand men in Judah; these were valiant men who were able to draw

the sword. No sooner had the work been accomplished than *"David's heart smote him,"* and he acknowledged his sin. The following morning, the prophet
Gad came to David and requested him to choose the
penalty that God would inflict upon him for his disobedience. The result was that God sent a pestilence
upon Israel, which caused the death of seventy thousand men. As the angel of the Lord continued to destroy Israel, the Lord repented Him of the evil and
said to the angel, *"It is enough: stay now thine hand."*
(v. 16). The Scriptures continue by saying, *"And the
angel of the Lord was by the threshing-place of
Araunah the Jebusite."* Gad came to David and instructed him to erect an altar unto the Lord, in the
threshing-floor of Araunah, and David did according
as he was told. When Araunah saw the king, he
bowed himself to the ground and asked the king why
he was there. David replied, *"To buy the threshing-
floor of thee, to build an altar unto the Lord, that the
plague may be stayed from the people."* (v. 21). So
David bought the threshing-floor, the oxen that
trampled the grain, and the instruments of wood that
were used in connection with the threshing, for fifty
shekels of silver—the price of atonement. (v. 24).
There David erected an altar and offered the oxen
for burnt offerings and peace offerings, and the chapter closes with the blessed words, *"And the plague
was stayed from Israel."* (v. 25). From this we see
the threshing-floor was a place of judgment for sin.
Likewise, the place where Ruth was to make her consecration and receive her cleansing, anointing, and
the wedding garment is the place where God would
judge the sin that was handed down through Adam's

race. Not only did Christ die *"to save his people from their sins"* through justification but John said, *"Behold, the Lamb of God, which taketh away the sin of the world"* through sanctification. Sin must be judged in the person of Jesus Christ.

There is one more blessed thought that I desire to give you concerning the threshing-floor of Araunah. II Chronicles 3:1 reads as follows, *"Then Solomon began to build the house of the Lord at Jerusalem in mount Moriah, where the Lord appeared unto David his father, in the place that David had prepared in the threshing-floor of Ornan, the Jebusite."* In this verse you will find three important facts: **First,** "the threshing-floor of Ornan" (Araunah, margin) was the place called mount Moriah. Here is where Abraham offered up his son Isaac, (Gen. 22); this pointed forward to the time when Christ would die upon the cross. **Second,** in this place the sin of David was judged and the penalty completely met in the fifty shekels of silver—the price of atonement, which is so wonderfully portrayed in the atonement money in Exodus 30:11-16. **Third,** on this very spot Solomon began to build the house of the Lord, which is typical of the house of God—the body of Christ—which is represented in Ruth. This body, the Church of Christ, is built on the basis of atonement, which was provided by God in offering up His only begotten Son, as a sacrifice for sin, portrayed in Abraham offering up his only son, Isaac, on mount Moriah. This threshing-floor covered acres of ground, which consisted of one large solid piece of rock. This rock then was the foundation rock of atonement that was able to support

Solomon's temple, meaning it would afford a place of worship for Israel. Hundreds of years later Christ said, *"Upon this rock I will build my church; and the gates of hell shall not prevail against it."* (Matt. 16:18).

II. THE PLACE OF OBTAINMENT.

The place of obtainment was at his feet. (v. 4). This speaks of consecration. She was dealing directly with Boaz, for Naomi said, *"He will tell thee what thou shalt do."* (v. 4). In order for a believer to secure the baptism of the Holy Spirit, there is a consecration demanded on his part. The believer will be instructed what condition he must meet by Christ Himself rather than by a lot of *"buzzers"* whispering in the ears of the seeker as is so often seen these days. In verse six it reads: *"And she went down."* That is the direction every one will go in spirit before they obtain full salvation from the Heavenly Boaz. It is an upward goal with a downward process. When we are humble, He will exalt us; when we are empty, He will fill us; when we are weak, He will strengthen us. The words, *"When Boaz had eaten and drunk, and his heart was merry,"* shows that the harvest feast was about over. He had entertained his maidens and servants as was their custom at the close of their wheat harvest. This harvest feast was a feast similar to our Thanksgiving Day, and the purpose of it was to praise God that He had visited Bethlehem with bread. When Boaz retired for the night, he lay down beside the pile of grain in order to protect his own property from thieves. In the same manner, our

Heavenly Boaz watches over His own to protect them from harm and danger. Under this division note—

A. THE INQUIRY MADE.

B. THE INVOCATION MINISTERED.

C. THE INFLUENCE MEASURED.

A. THE INQUIRY MADE. *"Who art thou?"* Boaz awakened at midnight to find Ruth in his presence. Boaz asked the question, *"Who art thou?"* To this Ruth replies, *"I am Ruth thine handmaid."* It was not Ruth, the Moabitess; nor Ruth, the stranger; nor Ruth, the Moabitish damsel, but it was *"Ruth thine handmaid."* She was an eligible candidate to obtain this blessed rest from the hands of Boaz, and spiritually speaking, it is being fulfilled during this dispensation of the Holy Spirit—*"On my servants and on my handmaidens I will pour out in those days of my Spirit; and they shall prophesy."* (Acts 2:18).

When Jacob sought the blessing, (Gen. 32:24-32), the angel of the Lord asked him, *"What is thy name?"* (v. 27). *"And he said, Jacob."* In the meaning of his name (heel grasper) we find expressed the very condition of his inward nature. Before Jacob could receive the blessing, he had to acknowledge his spiritual state. Some folks object to the word **"blessing,"** but you will notice Jacob said to the angel, *"I will not let thee go, except thou bless me."* (v. 26). What Jacob received that night was, in his own mind, a **"blessing."** The same thought is brought forth in the case of Esau—*"who for one morsel of meat sold his birthright. For ye know how that afterward, when*

*he would have inherited 'the blessing,' he was re-
jected."* (Heb. 12:16, 17).

There should be no objection to the term **"second
blessing."** Esau's birthright was one thing and parental blessing is another thing. Here two experiences are taught: **1st**, the *"birthright,"* which in
type foreshadows the new birth; **2nd**, the parental
"blessing," the *"promise of the Father,"* which is bestowed upon the sons and daughters in the Divine
Family by their Heavenly parent. This parental
blessing usually belonged to the first-born son, who
was entitled to a double portion of all his father's inheritance. (Deut. 21:15-17). This would enable him
to worthily represent the dead and maintain the hon-
or of his name. Elisha claimed this portion on the
grounds of sonship when twice he repeated the
words, *"My father."* (II Kings 2:12). He, therefore,
received the double portion from the hands of the
prophetical parent, Elijah, and in the power of the
spirit went forth and smote the Jordan, which *"part-
ed hither and thither: and Elisha went over."* The student will do well to read the second chapter of II
Kings in connection with this study. Immediately
following the study of Esau in Hebrews 12 we come
"unto mount Sion," which is the *"church of the first-
born."* (v. 23). This body of believers is entitled to
the baptism of the Holy Spirit, the parental blessing
from the hand of God the Father in the nature of a
double portion, in the same manner as the first-born
son received the double portion on the grounds of his
relationship as portrayed in the case of Elijah. This
is what Ruth was seeking for; in other words, it

could be called *"soul rest."*

B. THE INVOCATION MINISTERED. *"Blessed be thou of the Lord, my daughter: for thou hast shewed more kindness in the latter end than at the beginning, inasmuch as thou followedst not young men, whether poor or rich."* (v. 10). Boaz recognized her love for him, inasmuch as she had not followed the young men, whether they were poor or rich. The clamor and the society of the world had no more charms for Ruth than they do for twice-born men today. A Christian does not desire to follow the fashions of the poor or rich but instead desires to walk in the footsteps of the meek and lowly Nazarene (Jesus). In chapter 2, verse 11, Boaz makes a full confession of his knowledge of her complete separation from the land of Moab and the acceptance of a people who were strangers to her. But in this study he goes a step farther by blessing her for her kindness in remaining in his field of activity and service and not running off with the young men of the world. Again the truth of entire separation is taught. It is simply impossible to remain in fellowship and relationship with Christ and follow a Christ-rejecting world.

C. THE INFLUENCE MEASURED. *"All the city of my people doth know that thou art a virtuous woman."* (v. 11). She had not been in Bethlehem very long, but all the inhabitants of the city knew she was a woman with a pure character. This should at once remove all the question marks regarding Ruth's action in this chapter, for if we understand the Eastern custom of their day, the subject is much more easily understood. One of the writers on the Book of Ruth writes the following, which may explain, in a measure, Ruth's conduct: "It is an Oriental courtship, and strange and unbecoming as Ruth's conduct might appear in the eyes of Westerners, it was considered perfectly proper in the 'days when the judges ruled,' and would be considered so still in the East." C. Knapp. Another custom of that day was that if a man died and left no children, his nearest kinsman, perhaps the younger brother, was to marry the widow that the genealogy providing for the coming of the Messiah, (Jesus Christ), might be continued. Ruth had a perfect right according to the Mosaic law and Oriental custom to make a proposal to Boaz that she might preserve the genealogy and reclaim the mortgaged estate left by Elimelech. This thought will be clarified in our next study.

Ruth's proposal can be seen in the 9th verse where she says, *"Spread therefore thy skirt over thine handmaid; for thou art a near kinsman."* A comparison of this truth is found in Ezekiel 16:8 where God says, *"I spread my skirt over thee."* In this verse the relationship between Israel and God is pictured in the symbol of marriage. When God looked upon Israel, (v. 8), He saw her beauty. The time was a *"time of love,"* and God continues by saying, *"I spread my skirt over thee, and covered thy nakedness."* God entered into a covenant there with Israel, and the verse closes with these blessed words: "And thou becamest mine. The word *"skirt,"* in both of these passages referred to, is from the Hebrew word *"kanaph"* meaning *"wing."* The same Hebrew word is found in Ruth 2:12, where Boaz states *"under whose wings*

thou art come to trust." It signifies a place of covering and protection. Here then we see Ruth claiming
Boaz as the redeemer kinsman, a claim of union (marriage) with him, which was to give her the protection, inheritance, and fellowship, which she—a stranger in the land of Bethlehem—so longed for. In Ezekiel 16:8, the verse previously viewed, we see the engagement between Israel and God, but in the same
way, this proposal in the Book of Ruth marked the
engagement between Ruth and Boaz, typical of the
Gentile Church and Jesus Christ. Boaz comforts
Ruth by saying, *"Fear not; I will do to thee all that
thou requirest."* (v. 11). What a wonderful promise
for a seeking soul. We will now enter into the third
division of this present subject—

III. PENTECOSTAL OUTCOME. (v's. 13-18).

As Ruth lay at his feet, she is informed by Boaz
that there is one called the near kinsman, who stands
between her and Boaz, one that is keeping him from
accepting the proposal. This near kinsman will be
considered in the following chapter, which is full of
typical truth. Paul studied at the feet of Gamaliel and
became a great **student**. Mary wept at the feet of
Jesus and became a great **saint**. Ruth rested at the
feet of Boaz, and became a great **savior**, for she preserved the genealogy or seed-line which would trace
back to the tribe of Judah from which Jesus Christ
would descend. Under this main division, "PENTE-
COSTAL OUTCOME," let us note—

A. THE COMMANDING REQUEST.

B. THE COMPETENT RESOURCE.

C. THE COMFORTING RESULT.

A. THE COMMANDING REQUEST." *"Tarry this night."* (v. 13). The word *"tarry"* at once reminds us of another command to tarry, which was given by the Savior when He said to the apostles *"tarry ye in the city of Jerusalem, until ye be endued with power from on high."* (Luke 24:49). The word *"tarry,"* in this verse just quoted, is from the Greek word *"kathizo"* meaning *"to sit or set down,"* indicating a work accomplished, as previously explained. The one hundred and twenty were so obedient to the Savior's command that the Spirit records in Acts 2:2 their faithfulness to His command by saying, *"Suddenly there came a sound from heaven as of a rushing mighty wind, and it filled all the house where they were sitting."* It gives us the thought that these disciples were converted, the work of regeneration had been accomplished in their lives, and they were now ready for the infilling of the Holy Spirit. As the disciples were told to wait for the promise of the Father so Ruth was told to wait until the morning. It is always morning to the soul when any work or experience of redemption is performed. There were three outstanding occurrences that took place in the morning: **First,** when the resurrection occurred, which is typical of impartation of life, it was morning. When the disciples arrived at the empty tomb and found it vacant, this was a promise of new life for the world.

Second, when the one hundred and twenty disciples received the promise of the Father by the indwelling of the Holy Spirit at Pentecost, it was morning. There was such a display of power and demonstration that the Jews accused them of being intoxicated by saying, *"These men are full of new wine."* (Acts 2:13). But Peter explained that they were not drunk as the Jews supposed they were, for it was but the third hour, that is nine o'clock in the morning, and seldom did a religious Jew ever eat or drink before that hour, which was the hour of prayer. This shows that it was morning. The night had passed, and the day came forth with new power, new activity, and new hope. So it was in the life of Ruth.

Third, Peter at the Mount of Transfiguration gives us a prophetic teaching of the coming of the Lord Jesus Christ. There were three persons in the glory at the transfiguration of Christ. Christ was the central figure, and Moses and Elijah were with Him. Elijah, who was translated or raptured away, represented those who will be *"caught up"* without dying. Moses represents those who have fallen asleep but who will be raised in resurrection glory at the coming of the Lord. Peter declares that we have now a more sure word of prophecy than the prophetic teaching of the Mountain Experience. It is the Word of God. Wherefore, we are to take heed to the Word of God, which is as a light shining in a dark place and which will continue to do so until the **"day dawn"** (morning). (II Pet. 1:16-21). Here Peter likens the coming of the Lord to the **"day dawn."** In the Song of Solomon, we have the same thought presented in these words: "Until the **day break,** and the shadows flee away." (Chap. 2:17). Here is a picture of the rapture when Christ will call His bride home. *"Rise up, my love,*

*my fair one, and come away. For, lo, the winter is
past, the rain is over and gone; The flowers appear
on the earth; the time of the singing of birds is come,
and the voice of the turtle is heard in our land; The
fig tree putteth forth her green figs, and the vines
with the tender grape give a good smell. Arise, my
love, my fair one, and come away."* (v's. 10-13). What
a beautiful picture this gives. The long winter of sin
has come to a close; the rains of opposition and tur-
moil are over; the flowers of fragrance appear on the
earth; there is music of the birds filling the atmosphere; the voice of the turtle dove is heard in our
land, which represents the Holy Spirit brooding over
Palestine; the fig tree is bringing forth green figs,
which is a symbol of the Jewish nation taking on new
life. He closes with the 13th verse: *"Arise, my love,
my fair one, and come away."* From this we find that
all the works of redemption performed in the soul in
justification, sanctification, and glorification are likened to the morning.

B.   A COMPETENT RESOURCE. *"Six measures
of barley."* (v. 15). Boaz requested that she bring
the vail or the sheet (which was used for the evening
covering) into which he poured six measures of barley. These six measures of barley were the evidence
that Boaz was satisfied with Ruth. It was a token of
his acceptance. In like manner is the baptism of the
Holy Spirit to every believer. In study five, we find
Ruth had gleaned all day and at the close received an
ephah of barley, which was a ten days' supply. This
she received for working, but now she received six
measures of barley as her gift for waiting. Some folks

would much rather work than they would to wait.
They seem to have the idea that spiritual power and
victory depend on the amount of work they can do,
and they are busy baking, sewing, selling, or doing
something to help the "poor Lord" carry on His work.
But you will receive more by waiting on Him one
night than by working one month. This is the Pentecostal Outcome—six measures of barley. However,
the number six falls short of the perfect number,
seven, but there could not be complete and perfect
satisfaction until she received Boaz in marriage, the
seventh character in the Book, typical of Jesus Christ.
Boaz gave her this supply of barley for he would not
have her go empty to her mother-in-law. (v. 17).
You will not be empty if you spend a night at the
feet of your Heavenly Boaz. Again the dispensational
teaching is "we must remember the Jewish people."
Although Naomi (typical of the Jewish nation) came
back from Moab with the confession *the Lord hath
brought me home empty,*" Ruth, the Gentile, left the
feet of Boaz with the words ringing in her ears, *"Go
not empty unto thy mother-in-law."*

When Ruth returned, Naomi asked her the question, *"Who art thou, my daughter?"* (v. 16). She
meant by that, *"Are you still Ruth, the handmaid, or
are you now Ruth, the wife of Boaz?"* Some of these
days the trumpet will sound, and the saints will be
raptured home no longer to be the peculiar people in
the eyes of the world but to be exalted to a high
place, the bride of Christ.

C. THE COMFORTING RESULT. Ruth was requested by Naomi to *"sit still"* until she knew the outcome of the matter. There is a time for us to *"sit still,"* just as there was a time for Israel to *"stand still"* when they were confronting the Red Sea. One great writer has said, *"When you don't know what to do, do nothing."* Just wait on the Lord, sit still, and see Him work. Some people who have made a complete consecration and yet did not receive the baptism of the Spirit in their lives, have had to sit still and trust before God fulfilled His promise. Why must Ruth *"sit still"*? Naomi said, *"The man will not be in rest, until he have finished the thing this day."* He Who hath begun the work is able to finish it, but this finishing process can only be completed when that near kinsman, whom I spoke of, is set aside and the barriers removed. Naomi said, *"The man will not be in rest."* When God created the Heavens and earth and finished the creation of all things, He rested on the seventh day, but when Adam fell, His rest ended. Immediately God began to work; it was a work of redemption to redeem lost men. It is seen in the act of God in clothing the guilty pair with the skins of animals, which portrayed the shedding of blood. Down through the centuries God, Christ, and the Holy Spirit have been busy at work to redeem lost men that eventually they might rest in the wonderful work of redemption. After Jesus healed the impotent man in John 5, the Jews found fault with Him because He had performed a miracle on the Sabbath Day. The Sabbath spoke of rest, which God had provided for the human body. Jesus in reply to their accusations said, *"My father worketh hitherto, and I work."* That is, up to that time, God had continued to work, and now Christ joins hands with Him, and they are jointly working for the salvation of lost men. Since then the Holy Spirit descended at Pentecost and has united with the Father and Son to continue in the work of redemption. The work must be finished *"this day."* This is the day of salvation, and God cannot rest as long as men are going on in sin and are possessed with evil hearts.

DAVID AND THE REDEEMER

STUDY SEVEN

(Ruth 4:1-22)

In our first study we found Naomi and Ruth in a state of **degradation.** The main thought was the famine and the failure. In the second lesson the main theme was **renunciation.** There we saw the decision and the departure. In study number three the key word was **regeneration.** The leading thought was contrition and confession. In the fourth lesson Ruth entered into a life of new **occupation.** There we saw her activity and advancement. In study five we found the key word was **remuneration.** Ruth was at work gleaning in the field, and was given handfuls on purpose. The scope of that lesson can be summed up in two words, the kinsman and his kindness. In study number six the main teaching and key word was **sanctification.** Raiment and rest are the two words that cover the chapter. This present study (number seven) gives the **typical** teaching of the Marriage of the Lamb, the key word being **glorification.** The chapter ends with the thought of marriage and the mother. Thus, we have the seven studies with their key words and main thoughts, which cover verse by verse, the Book of Ruth.

THE KINSMAN REDEEMER

I will now give a brief explanation of the threefold work of the kinsman redeemer, fulfilled in Boaz, which points forward to Jesus Christ, the Redeemer

of the world. The work of the kinsman redeemer
was as follows:

FIRST. **To Redeem from Bondage.** (Lev. 25:47-
50). In these verses you will notice that if a brother
became poor and sold himself to a stranger or so-
journer, one of his brethren or near kinsmen could
redeem him *"if he be able"* to do so. This lesson
gives us a spiritual picture of the Garden of Eden,
where Adam was sold *"unto sin"* by his own hand,
and thus entered into poverty and bondage. The
"stranger" that bought him into slavery was Satan,
who subtly deceived Adam and Eve until they were
brought into physical, spiritual, and mental bondage.
Ever since then the human race has been in slavery.
Men are slaves to their appetites, to pride, to cursing,
dishonesty, and hundreds of other things. A man,
like the Jewish nation, may claim his freedom by
saying, *"We be Abraham's seed, and were never in
bondage to any man."* (John 8:33). However, the
fact remains: the natural man is a slave. At the
very time that the Jews made this statement, they
were in national bondage to Caesar of Rome. At
that time Christ tried to impress upon their minds
that if He would make them free they would be free
indeed. (John 8:36). It takes Christ, Him alone to
deliver us from spiritual bondage, from the hand of
the stranger to whom we have been sold.

In these verses we are now discussing the person
who was to redeem must be *"nigh of kin."* Lev. 25:
49). In order that Jesus could be our near kinsman,
He had to become our elder brother and take upon
Himself the *"seed of Abraham,"* and *"to be made like
unto his brethren."* (Heb. 2:16, 17). It further states

in Leviticus that *"He shall reckon with him that bought him from the year that he was sold to him until the year of jubilee."* (Lev. 25:50). Jesus Christ reckoned with this stranger (Satan) on Calvary to redeem the human race from the year that Adam was sold into sin or from the beginning of the fall of man until the year of jubilee, which is typical of the Ages of Ages, spoken of in Ephesians 2:7. Christ reckoned, that is, paid the penalty that would cover this period of time.

It also says (speaking of the man that is sold in bondage): *"If he be able, he may redeem himself."* (v. 49). There is one little word that stands in the way of this man redeeming himself; that is the word *"if," "if he be able."* David saw the impossibility of this when he said, *"They that trust in their wealth, and boast themselves in the multitude of their riches; None of them can by any means redeem his brother, nor give to God a ransom for him: (For the redemption of their soul is precious, and it ceaseth for ever)."* (Psalm 49:6-8). Jesus added to this when He said, *"What shall a man give in exchange for his soul?"* (Matt. 16:26). There is only one power in the world that can break the spiritual bondage that now grips the human race—that is the power of the Gospel through the Son of God.

SECOND. **To Redeem from Poverty.** Lev. 25: 25-28). In these verses we find the law of the kinsman redeemer relative to poverty. If one of the Israelites had become poor and he had sold his earthly possessions, his near kinsman could redeem them for him. If the kinsman or Israelite was not able to restore it to him, then that which was sold was to remain in pos-

session of the man who held the mortgage. That was
the law of poverty. Not only did Adam sell himself
into spiritual bondage and forfeit his liberty, but his
earthly possessions—the Garden of Eden—and the
universe was also sold into the hands of Satan. From
this we see that man and earth fall and rise together.
As they are closely connected in creation so they are,
provisionally, united in redemption. Thus the old
world lies in poverty while the human race has been
forced into bankruptcy. The law providing that the
kinsman redeemer could buy back this mortgaged
estate and property was a law for the poor and not
for the rich. For that reason Jesus said, *"The poor
have the gospel preached to them."* In giving the
laws of the Kingdom, (Matt. 5:3), Jesus said, *"Blessed are the poor in spirit: for theirs is the kingdom of
heaven."* When a man acknowledges his poverty, is
willing to enter into spiritual bankruptcy, admits
that he has nothing with which to redeem himself,
and confesses he is sold into the hands of the stranger,
the near Kinsman is ready to buy back the mortgage
that rests upon his own spirit and upon the spiritual
property that he possesses. When a person becomes
independent, he doesn't want God. Such is the condition of the Laodicean church, who say, *"I am rich
. . . and have need of nothing."* Yet Jesus reminds
them that they are poor and counsels them to buy of
Him, His gold, His eyesalve, and His raiment. (Rev.
3:17, 18). "Yes, Jesus, our near Kinsman, is able to
buy back that which we have lost with His wealth,
called 'the unsearchable riches of Christ.'" (Eph.
3:8). He is rich in mercy, (Eph. 2:4); He is rich in
grace, (Eph. 1:7); and He is rich in glory, (Eph. 3:

16). With His mercy, grace, and glory, He is able to
buy back our lost inheritance.

THIRD. **To Redeem from the Dead.** (Deut. 25:5,
6). Thus far, we have seen our Kinsman Redeemer
buying back the lost liberty and possessions of man.
Yet there is one more duty for the kinsman to perform; that was to redeem the name of the dead. For
that reason, Ruth, the Gentile, was to marry Boaz
that not only the lost property might be restored to
Ruth, but also *"to raise up the name of the dead,"*
Mahlon. (Ruth 4:10). S. Ridout in his book on
Ruth writes, "In Israel, to be childless was a reproach, and for a man's name to be blotted out—his
family to become extinct—was regarded as a special
mark of God's displeasure." He further continues,
"There seems, too, to be a recognition in His provision of that hope in the heart of every Hebrew
woman, that through her in some way the promise of
'the woman's seed' might be fulfilled. This was to be
done literally in the line which was to be preserved
through Ruth." God had a purpose in this because
He wanted the genealogy to continue that out of it
might come Jesus Christ, the near Kinsman. The
provision of the law was to preserve the name of the
dead, which would be on this order: If a man by
the name of Judah would die, leaving no children,
the near kinsman who was able should marry his
widow, and their first-born son was to carry on the
genealogy and preserve the name of the departed
dead. It gives us the thought that though we be
dead, we live on. Philip Mauro so beautifully writes,
"We gather that the chief lesson taught by this fea-

ture of God's wonderful law is that God is greater
than death, that He is ever the God of Abraham 'Who
quickeneth the dead and calleth those things which
be not as though they were,' and that after death has
done its worst, God can bring back the dead again,
and place them, more securely than ever, 'in the lot
of their inheritance.' " He continues, "If we look in
a comprehensive way at the work which the Son of
God undertook when He stooped to assume the relation of near Kinsman, or Redeemer, to the perishing
human race, we can readily see that it embraced, indeed, individual salvation (that is, deliverance of
persons and restoration of goods), for all who trust
in Him; but that it also contemplated, as it were, the
recovery and restoration of man's inheritance (the
earth) and the bringing back of the human family
itself from the dead, and the placing of that family,
fully restored in every way from the effects of sin
and death, upon their inheritance, to enjoy it forever!" Thank God, provisions have been made to
restore a condemned race, a cursed earth, and a
crushed hope.

REDEMPTION BY THE REDEEMER

The word *"redemption,"* according to Robert
Young, has various meanings such as *"to free, to separate, to loose, or to buy with a price."* The word
"mortgage" is from the French words *"mort"* meaning *"death,"* and *"gage"* meaning *"pledge,"* so a
mortgage is a death pledge. (Webster). When a
piece of property is mortgaged a death pledge is
signed. If this mortgage is not paid in full at the appointed time, the property must be forfeited to the

one holding the mortgage. Likewise, when Adam sinned, he mortgaged the universe, and a death pledge fell upon both the earth and the human race. *"For all have sinned, and come short of the glory of God."* If property is mortgaged, another has a claim to it as long as that mortgage exists. Likewise, with the fallen race and the universe, another — the *"stranger,"* the devil—had a claim on it, but there came a time of settlement when not only the mortgage but the taxes and interest had to be accounted for, and the total amount paid up in full. Someone—that Someone was Jesus Christ—went to the cross of Calvary, took the accumulated sins and transgressions from the beginning of the Adamic race and the mortgage held by Satan, and made a payment in full, canceling the debt so that Satan no longer could have a claim on those who desired to be free. After a mortgage comes due, there is still a period of time, called *"a time of grace."* During that time something decisive must be done. We are now in that period of grace, and although the penalty has been accounted for and the price of redemption paid, something decisive must be done on man's part in order for him to be free from the domineering hand of Satan. He must go to Him, Who has paid the redemptive price, and claim Him as his Redeemer. Over four thousand years went by and the mortgage became due, but the Son of God, the near Kinsman Redeemer, came down from Heaven and paid the old debt, all the accumulated acts of transgression and sin from the beginning of time, and He is now waiting to remove them from the records as man makes the application.

It has often been the case in business transactions that the person who has lost the property is not willing to vacate. In such cases the sheriff must remove by force the occupant and his belongings from the premises. In a similar way, Satan will refuse to give up his possession of the earth, but Jesus Christ, Who will act as the sheriff of the universe, will remove the occupant and all his possessions, such as sin, the curse, demons, and Christ-rejecters from the premises and lock them in the bottomless pit. Then, as one has said, "He will give the keys to the Sadducees, who do not believe in a resurrection." Satan knows his time is short and at present is working over time with large forces to retain the possessions on this earth. For that reason, he is using severe methods on the child of God, for he would drive all holiness and righteousness from the earth that he may be the sole possessor. Nearly two thousand years ago the Prince of this World was judged, and at present he is out on bail, waiting for the final execution of the sentence. The Redeemer Kinsman has met, in every particular, the claims of him who held the mortgage, including the accumulated interest and taxes, and with the price of redemption, which was His own blood, has made full atonement so that on the grounds of faith in His accomplished work, man can be free.

I. **REDEEMED AT THE GATE.**

II. **RESTORED GENTILES.**

III. **RESULT OF GENEALOGY.**

I. **REDEEMED AT THE GATE.**

"Then went Boaz up to the gate, and sat him down there." (Chap. 4:1). The gate was the place where decisions were made, where judgment was meted out, similar to a court room of today. There all the business of the people of Israel was transacted. There matters were settled and judgment placed upon the same. One author has called it *"a judgment place."* How this reminds us of Jesus, Who went outside the city walls of Jerusalem and *"suffered without the gate."* (Heb. 13:12). It was there that He transacted the spiritual matters relating to a lost world, the people of Israel, and the Church of the living God. It was a place of judgment; there sin was judged. He, Who knew no sin, was made sin for us that we might be made the righteousness of God. (II Cor. 5:21). Jesus described this gate as strait and narrow, and urged men to *"enter in at the strait gate."* (Matt. 7: 13). He did this because He knew judgment was coming on the human race, and He, Himself, must bear the judgment at the place appointed—outside the gate. Let us note the classes of people at the gate:

A. THE TEN ELDERS. (v. 2). Ten in Scriptures is the number of responsibility as seen on page 116. Here there were ten elders, which were representative of the law. As the law was interested in the transaction of Boaz at the gate of Bethlehem so the law was interested in the judgment meted out on Calvary at the gate of Jerusalem. Why was this? The law says that *"the soul that sinneth, it shall die,"* and Jesus became sin for us that we might be made the righteousness of God. Therefore, the penalty of sin, which was meted out by the law, rested upon Jesus Christ in those hours of agony and suffering as He was passing out from a life of sacrifice to a life of intercession. The law was interested in the cross of Christ because He took the penalty of the broken law for mankind. Man in his natural state could not keep the law, but Christ not only kept it but fulfilled it. Therefore the law (the ten commandments) are no longer in force for the Christian because Christ nailed them to the cross. This is plainly taught in the third chapter of second Corinthians. The law we now have is not ten commandments, but two, which are: *"And thou shalt love the Lord thy God with all thy heart, and with all thy soul, and with all thy mind, and with all thy strength: this is the first commandment. And the second is like, namely this, Thou shalt love thy neighbour as thyself."* (Mark 12:30, 31). The elders were at the gate to witness that all that Boaz did was done honestly and correctly. Likewise, Jesus was closely observed during His earthly career.

The testimony of the Word of God as to His attitude toward sin in His earthly life is threefold. (1) His **character.** *"In him is no sin."* (I John 3:5). He had a holy character and was a righteous man. (2) His **conduct.** *"Who did no sin."* (I Pet. 2:22). Because of a holy character, He had a holy conduct and obeyed the law in every particular. (3) His **cognizance.** *"Who knew no sin."* (II Cor. 5:21). Because of this threefold fact, He was the Lamb without blemish, Who made perfect atonement for mankind that the penalty of the law might be met in Him and that the righteousness of the law might be fulfilled in us. As

the ten elders were at the gate to judge the transactions of the redemption between Boaz and Ruth
so the law of God stood at Mount Calvary to judge
the transaction of redemption accomplished by Jesus
Christ for the human race. This is plainly brought
out in Paul's letter to the Romans where he states:
*"But now the righteousness of God without the law
is manifested, being witnessed by the law."* (Chap.
3:21). Now this blessed righteousness possessed by
Jesus Christ is imparted to the individual who comes
to Him for redemption. He then can say with Paul
of old that the life that he now lives is not his own,
for it is no longer he that liveth but Christ Who
dwelleth in him. The supernatural change that is
seen in a twice-born man is wrought by the righteousness of Christ imparted into the life of the believer, causing him to live righteously.

B. THE PEOPLE. *"All the people that were in
the gate."* (v. 11). *"The people"* speaks of the world at
large. This group was also represented at Calvary.
*"All the people came together to that sight, be-
holding the things which were done, smote their
breasts."* (Luke 23:48). The last time the world (*the
people*) saw Jesus was on the cross; they never saw
Him in resurrection glory. The last look they had of
Him, pictured Him hanging on the cross, taking their
penalty, enduring the shame, but meeting the claims
of God that they might be free. This constantly reminds the world that the wages of sin is death. Six
(which is the world number) people testified: First,
as to His **identity**. The centurion said, *"Truly this
was the Son of God."* (Matt. 27:54). Although
throughout His ministry He claimed His divinity, His

crucifiers still doubted and in mockery challenged Him, as the Son of God, to come down from the cross. Second, as to the **imputation.** Pilate and Herod both said, *"I find no fault in Him.'* (Luke 23:14, 15). The word *"fault"* is from the Greek word *"aition,"* meaning *"I find no cause or case against Him."* Third, as to His **innocency.** Judas, the betrayer, casting the thirty shekels of silver at the feet of the chief priest, confessed *"I have betrayed the innocent blood."* (Matt. 27:4). The word *"innocent"* means *"to be guiltless."* Pilate uses the same word in the 24th verse where he states, *"I am innocent (guiltless) of the blood of this just person."* Fourth, as to His **integrity.** *"Have thou nothing to do with that just man."* (Matt. 27:19). These are the words of Pilate's wife in a message sent to Pilate warning him to have nothing to do with the crucifixion of Jesus, for He was a **"just man."** The word *"just"* is the same Greek word *"dikaios"* found in II Peter 2:7, 8 where it speaks of Lot as a *"righteous man."* Fifth, His **infallibility.** One of the thieves hanging on the cross near Christ confessed in his dying hour these words: *"We receive the due reward of our deeds: but this man hath done nothing amiss."* (Luke 23:41). The word *"amiss"* is translated by Young *"out of place."* This then should read: *"This man hath done nothing 'out of place'. "* This is the unconscious testimony of the people concerning Jesus Christ as He stood at the gate of Jerusalem, the place of judgment where He met the requirements and penalty of a broken law.

C. NAOMI AND RUTH. Naomi and Ruth were

found among those at the gate. Likewise the Jew and Gentile, typified by Naomi and Ruth, were gathered around the cross. Those who were at enmity were made friends, yes, relatives by the cross of Christ, for the middle wall of partition was broken down, as explained in a previous chapter. Now a Jew and a Gentile can live together in harmony. If under that dispensation, Ruth could dwell with her mother-in-law, I am sure that under grace the same harmony should prevail in the church today. How often strife has entered into congregations, causing many to become indifferent and backslidden in heart, destroying the church's influence, and spelling destruction for many souls.

D. THE UNNAMED KINSMAN. His name is not given, but he stood between Boaz and Ruth. Boaz wanted to marry Ruth. This desire he had in his heart, but the unnamed kinsman stood in his way, thus hindering his plans. Who was this kinsman? It was someone to whom was offered the opportunity to redeem the lost estate and marry Ruth but who was unable to do it. Some say it was a neighbor, but that is contradictory to both the Old Testament law and to typology. Psalm 49:7 proves the incongruity of that: *"None of them can by any means redeem his brother, nor give to God a ransom for him."* Some people believe it was an angel. They are ministering servants sent forth to minister to those who are heirs of salvation, (Heb. 1:14), but they were not able to redeem the fallen race. The unnamed kinsman surely couldn't represent the law, for it was engraved on tables of stone. It was inanimate; this was a person, a man at the gate. If it was a kinsman, it had to be a living person.

Philip Mauro gives, I believe, the correct interpretation of this near kinsman in his book on Ruth. He writes, "Surely, then, if Boaz is a figure of the New Man, by Whom the work of Redemption has been accomplished, and Who magnified the Law and made it honorable, then the 'nearer kinsman' is a figure of the 'old man,' who is of the earth, earthly, and who, when tested by the law of God, was manifested as a failure in respect to every requirement thereof. The 'old man' was our next of kin; and to him pertained in the first instance the right, and also the obligation, to redeem the inheritance." As the first Adam was of the earth, earthly, so the second Adam, Jesus Christ, is the Lord from Heaven, Heavenly. You will notice the two natures; one earthly and the other Heavenly or spiritual. The old man was of nearer kin to us than the Lord from Heaven because He was earthly. His disposition and desires can be plainly seen in this fourth chapter of Ruth when he said, *"I cannot redeem it for myself, lest I mar mine own inheritance."* (v. 6). The thought in his mind was *"mine own";* he lived for self. He wanted the land but not the lady; he desired money but not marriage. This is a picture of the old man in his true state, for his big ambition is selfish gain. *"I must come first,"* says he. *"I think more of myself and my inheritance than I do of the dead."* As the near kinsman was a barrier between Ruth and Boaz so the old man stands between Christ and the Christian.

It is this self life that stands in the way; wants to have pre-eminence and first place; desires to be notic-

ed and respected; wants to run the official board, the
church or the pastor; wants to be looked up to, as a
dictator or overseer. It's that proud and exalted principle within the human breast, which is often unfor-
giving, dogmatic, demonstrative and loud, but never
tender. That is what Christ desires to crucify, the old
man. After that is done, one can say with Paul, *"I am
crucified with Christ: nevertheless I live; yet not I,
but Christ liveth in me."* (Gal. 2:20). This obstacle
that stands in the way of perfect union can be removed, for Christ went to the cross and by His suffering, death, and resurrection made full atonement, not
only for the *sins* of the world but also for the *"sin of
the world."* Christ did not only die for what we did,
but also for what we are. This is taught by Paul in his
letter to the Romans: *"God sending his own Son in
the likeness of sinful flesh, and for sin* (by a sacrifice
for sin, margin), *condemned sin in the flesh."* (Chap.
8:3). Dr. Handley Moule, the great English expositor,
in his book on Romans treats this verse in the following manner: " **'And as sin-offering'**; expiatory and
reconciling, **'sentenced sin in the flesh'**; not pardoned
it, observe, but sentenced it. He orders it to execution; He kills its claim and its power for all who are
in Christ."

The work of Christ in atonement for **"sin"** is plainly taught in the sin-offering of Leviticus, chapter 4.
There is a difference between the trespass-offering
and the sin-offering. The trespass-offering was for
what we did, the sin-offering was for what we are. In
the sin-offering the fat, the kidneys, the caul, above
the liver, were all burned upon the brazen altar as
God's portion. This typified that the inward life of

the sacrifice (Jesus Christ) was pleasing and acceptable to God. The fat spoke of the richness of His grace. There were six items numerated in this chapter on the sin-offering, which was carried without the camp and burned upon the earth. (1) **The skin.** This was typical of the outer life of man. (2) **The flesh.** This was typical of his fallen nature. One has said, "In my flesh dwelleth no good thing." (3) **The head.** Man in his sinful state has a depraved mind, and his thoughts are evil continually. Satan has blinded his mind, that he might not see God. (4) **The legs.** Man in his unredeemed state has a sinful walk and needs to be shod with the preparation of the gospel of peace and as Asher *"Let him dip his foot in oil,"* (Deut. 33:24), that his walk might be under the anointing of the Holy Ghost. (5) **The inwards.** The natural man's inner life is vile and full of sin. (6) **The dung.** All that he feeds on is refuse and is only fit for the draught. (Mark 7:19). These six items (one short of the perfect number seven) had to be removed outside the camp and burned, showing that a man in his fallen depraved state needs a complete atonement for transgressions and for sin; otherwise, he is separated from God outside of the camp, as the leper, who was barred from the fellowship and as the Sabbath-breaker, who was stoned for disobedience.

Outside of the atonement there is nothing left for man but death. Man stands not only in need of the justifying but also the sanctifying grace of God, as is seen by these two offerings. As the sin-offering was burned without the camp so Boaz had to go without the gate, the place of judgment, and purchase the lost property and redeem Ruth for his wife, thereby setting aside the nearer kinsman. In the same way Christ suffered without the camp or gate of Jerusalem, *"that he might sanctify the people with his own blood."* (Hebrews 13:12). The old man had four thousand years in which to redeem himself, but he was unable to do it and had to yield to the demands of another, the Lord from Heaven. We can now say with Paul, *"Knowing this, that our old man is crucified with him* (Jesus) *that the body of sin might be destroyed,* (by consent of the believer), *that henceforth we should not serve sin."* (Rom. 6:6).

THE SHOE AND THE REPROACH

In Deuteronomy 25:7-10 we find the law relative to this near kinsman. If this nearer kinsman would refuse to take his brother's wife in marriage, to raise up the name of the dead, and preserve the seedline, then the widow could make her complaint to the elders of the city, who in turn would judge this man at the gate (the place of judgment). If he would then continue to refuse to meet the requirements of the law, he was to surrender the shoe from off his foot, and she, in turn, was to spit in his face. These two acts teach the surrender of his power and the reproach of his name. This reproach was to be handed down to his offspring and the coming generations. This law was enforced at the gate of Bethlehem in the transaction between the near kinsman and Boaz when the man plucked off his shoe as the evidence of surrender and reproach. Therefore, all who live in sin today must in the same manner bear the reproach that sin brings. However, all those who are living in Jesus

Christ, as Israel at Gilgal, have the reproach of Egypt (the world and sin) rolled away, for He bore the reproach outside the gate, when they spit in His face and three days later in His resurrection Christ plucked off the graveclothes as a token that the covenant was sealed and the inheritance redeemed. Yes, thank God, He has broken the bars of sin and death asunder and now stands a complete victor.

II. RESTORED GENTILES.

Boaz now calls the ten elders and the people and says, *"Ye are witnesses this day,* that I have bought all that was Elimelech's." (v. 9). Note the term **"this day."** Naomi informed Ruth that the man would not be in rest until he had finished the **thing** *"this day."* (Chap. 3:12). Today, *"this day"* referred to, is the day of grace. Christ will not be at rest until perfect, complete salvation has been wrought in the lives of His bride, of which Ruth is a type. Because **"this day"** in which we are now living is the day of grace, the Holy Spirit is seeking to give to every believer the soul rest provided in the atonement of Jesus Christ, thereby removing the nearer kinsman in preparation for the Marriage of the Lamb.

Boaz further adds, *"Ruth the Moabitess, the wife of Mahlon, have I purchased to be my wife."* (v. 10). What beautiful language here expresses the work of Jesus Christ on the cross. It is called a *"purchase."* The same thought is brought forth in Ephesians 1:14 where the church is called the *"purchased possession."* The ten elders and the people testify to the transactions by saying, *"We are witnesses."* (v. 11). In the same manner, Peter and the apostles answered

the magistrates at Jerusalem by saying, *"We are witnesses of these things."* (Acts 5:29-32). The emphasis
is on the words *"these things."* There were four acts
mentioned, in those verses, of which they were witnesses. (1) **The death of Christ.** "Ye slew and hanged
on a tree." It is substitution; Christ died for us. (2)
The resurrection of Christ. "The God of our Fathers
raised up Jesus." Here we have restoration—restor-
ing of Divine life to the soul. (3) **The exaltation of
Christ.** "Him hath God exalted with his right hand
to be a Prince and a Saviour." He had humbled himself, but He is now raised to the highest heights in
glory. (4) **The work of Christ.** "For to give repentance to Israel, and forgiveness of sins." Here we
have reconciliation. Christ reconciles men because
of their repentance and His forgiveness. They were
witnesses to this fourfold truth of Christ—His death,
His resurrection, His exaltation, and His work. Let
us note the threefold blessing pronounced upon Ruth
by the witnesses—

A. RECEIVING POWER IN EPHRATAH. *"Do
thou worthily* (get thee power, margin) *in Ephratah."*
(v. 11). Ephratah is just another name for Bethlehem. As Boaz retained his influential power in his
community so hundreds of years later there was born
in this village One, Who was able by His power to
transform lives and make men walk as He walked.
1st, Jesus had saving power. Paul said, *"For I am not
ashamed of the gospel of Christ: for it is the power
of God unto salvation."* (Rom. 1:16). **2nd,** it is en-
duing power. Jesus said, *"Tarry ye in the city of
Jerusalem, until ye be endued with power from on*

high." (Luke 24:49). **3rd,** it is glorifying power. *"God hath both raised up the Lord, and will also raise up us by his own power."* (I Cor. 6:14).

B. PROCLAIMING THE NAME IN BETHLEHEM. *"Be famous* (proclaim thy name, margin) *in Bethlehem."* (v. 11). Boaz obtained a great name because of his willingness to marry the wife of Mahlon and thus continue the lineage that came from the tribe of Judah so that out of it David, the king, and Christ, the Saviour, might come. In the same manner our Heavenly Boaz, Jesus, obtained a great name in Bethlehem when He was born on that memorable day; they said, *"Thou shalt call his name JESUS: for he shall save his people from their sins."* (Matt. 1:21). A name, which is above every name; it is a universal name, used in every country, in every climate, and in every class. Even devils acknowledge His name, for when the demoniac who resided in tombs came face to face with Christ, he said, *"What have I to do with thee, Jesus, thou Son of the most high God?"* (Mark 5:7). He acknowledged there both His humanity and His divinity, for the name, Jesus, is always used when it refers to His humanity. How blessed that name is to every believer. No wonder Mrs. Lydia Baxter wrote—

> Take the name of Jesus with you,
> Child of sorrow and of woe;
> It will joy and comfort give you,
> Take it, then, where'er you go.

C. HAVING A HOUSE LIKE PHAREZ. They continue their blessing—*"Let thy house be like the house of Pharez."* (v. 12). Pharez was a son of Judah and Tamar, from whom came the largest tribe of all the twelve. Although this house was numbered to the amount of *"threescore and sixteen thousand and five hundred,"* (Num. 26:22), there is still a larger house than this one. While the house of Pharez could be numbered, the house of God, which came out of Boaz and Ruth, is innumerable. John says the *"number of them was ten thousand times ten thousand, and thousands of thousands."* (Rev. 5:11).

III. RESULT OF GENEALOGY. (v's. 13-22).

This division of our study covers the last few verses of this wonderful Book of Ruth, which contains far more truth than what appears from a first reading. There is much more that we could write than has already been written, but time and the size of the book forbids it. In these closing verses let us note—

A. THE BETROTHAL AND THE MARRIAGE.

B. THE BLESSING AND THE MOTHER.

C. THE BIRTHRIGHT AND THE MANGER.

A. THE BETROTHAL AND THE MARRIAGE. (v. 13). When Ruth tarried at his feet, (chap. 3:13, 14), it was night, but the morning has arrived. Complete redemption has been secured, and the marriage is to take place. The betrothal was made in the night at the feet of Boaz. She made her complete preparation then by the washing, the anointing, and the clothing (the wedding garment). (Chap. 3:3). No doubt, it seemed a long time for her to wait for the breaking of the day, but at last the hour has arrived. Her heart leaps for joy as she knows that she, a stranger and a Gentile, is to have the wealthy kinsman as her bridegroom. So it is with us in this dispensation. It is night; our preparation is being made for the Marriage of the Lamb. We must be washed, anointed, and clothed—ready for the daybreak when we shall rise to meet our wealthy Kinsman and Redeemer in the air, there to be ushered into the presence of angels, cherubims, Old Testament saints, and patriarchs, yea, into the presence of God to be united in marriage to Jesus Christ. Such is the dispensational picture of this Book. As I dictate these lines, how my heart thrills with hope to think of the prospects that lie in the near future.

The term *"marriage"* reminds us of Genesis 2:18 when God said, *"It is not good that the man should be alone; I will make him an help meet for him."* After God had made Eve from one of the ribs of Adam, He presented her to him as his bride. After Adam received her, he said, *"This is now bone of my bones, and flesh of my flesh."* (v. 23). In the same manner, Jesus will welcome us into His presence, for we too *"are members of his body, of his flesh, and of his bones."* (Eph. 5:30). After the union of Adam and Eve, God laid down the rule for marriage by saying, *"Therefore shall a man leave his father and his mother, and shall cleave unto his wife: and they shall be one flesh."* Paul quotes nearly the same words in the chapter in Ephesians just referred to, verse 31. It is in this chapter that he pictures the union between Christ and the Church, and he uses the husband and wife as a figure to describe the great event that is yet to take place. This wonderful union is described in the words *"they two shall be one flesh."*

THE NUMBER ONE

Here we find the number one. It expresses Divine
unity, supremacy, and independency. One writer describes it as "sufficiency, which needs no other, and
an independency which admits no other." The main
thought of the numeral is unity and harmony. It is
the number used to denote the Trinity—three in one
and one in three. *"The Lord our God is one Lord."*
(Deut. 6:4). Some may ask in derision, *"How can
three be one?"* My reply is in the nature of a question: *"How can two be one?"* How can man and wife,
two individual persons, be one flesh? The denial of
the Trinity, which has been very prominent in modernistic ranks, has crept into what is called the Pentecostal movement today—those who believe in *"Jesus
Only."* Paul writes: *"For through him (Jesus) we
both have access (Jew and Gentile) by one spirit unto the Father."* (Eph. 2:18). There you will notice the
three persons of the Trinity. Peter in writing to the
strangers scattered abroad calls them the *"elect according to the foreknowledge of God the Father,
through sanctification of the Spirit unto obedience
and sprinkling of the blood of Jesus Christ."* (I Pet.
1:2). With such Scripture facing us, how can men
deny the existence of a personal triune God?

Silly Billy, a feeble-minded lad, sat in a meeting
one night where they were discussing the doctrine of
the Trinity. Some of the wise and prudent men of the
congregation, to their amusement, saw that he was
taking notes. At the close of the service, they approached him, requesting that he show them his notes

that he had taken on this subject. On the sheet of paper, which he handed them, they found these words—

> "This can Silly Billy see:
> Three in one,
> And one in three,
> And one of them has died for me."

Seemingly Silly Billy could reason out these truths better than some of our so-called Bible students of today. The portion of Scripture found in Isaiah 35:8, *"But it shall be for those: the wayfaring men, though fools, shall not err therein,"* belonged to Silly Billy. Although he might have been rather dumb in the sight of some of those *"wise men"* at the convention, yet he had reasoning power enough to see that there was one God, composed of three persons.

The harmony and unity of the Church is found in the writings of Paul to the Ephesians where he states "There is **one** body, and **one** Spirit, even as ye are called in **one** hope of your calling; **One** Lord, **one** faith, **one** baptism, **One** God and Father of all, who is above all, and through all, and in you all." (Chap. 4: 4-6). Here you will find a sevenfold description of the unity of the Church, all described by the word *"one,"* found seven times. One, independent of any other number, also expresses the beginning or the origin of things. As it's the number of God, we see that all things begin with Him. Thus, the typical picture of the marriage of Ruth and Boaz is that we shall be one in harmony and unity throughout the countless ages of eternity.

B. THE BLESSING AND THE MOTHER. (v's. 14-17). In due time Ruth gave birth to a son, (v.

13), and the women of Bethlehem were so pleased
with the newcomer that they began to bless the
Lord for His kindness. The blessing indicated that
Naomi would be the benefactor throughout the life
of this child. *"He shall be unto thee (Naomi) a re-*
storer of thy life, and a nourisher of thine old age."
(v. 15). From a dispensational viewpoint, we can
see how this will come true through the child Jesus,
Who was born hundreds of years later. He shall be
a restorer of life and a nourisher to the Jewish people
in their old age. This will take place in the millennium.

In the last chapter of Genesis, we see how Joseph's
brethren came to him and sought forgiveness of the
sins they had committed in selling him to the Ishmae-
lites. This so affected Joseph that he wept before
them and said, *"Fear not: for am I in the place of*
God?" (v. 19). That means: *"I am in the place*
where God would have me be." He continues, *"God*
meant it unto good, to bring to pass, as it is this day,
to save much people alive. Now therefore hear ye
not: I will nourish you, and your little ones. And he
comforted them, and spake kindly unto them." (v's.
20, 21). In the same manner, the Jewish nation in
the latter days will fall down before Jesus in repentance and will seek forgiveness from the hand of
God because of their sin and their attitude in the
past. When they see the wounds in His hands, they
will ask, *"What are these wounds in thine hands?"*
To this Jesus will reply, *"Those with which I was*
wounded in the house of my friends." (Zech. 13:6).
What pathetic language! The great day of atonement will come again for the remnant of Israel. *"In*

*that day there shall be a fountain opened to the house
of David and to the inhabitants of Jerusalem for sin
and for uncleanness."* (Zech. 13:1). That has a
deeper meaning than just the cross of Christ for this
dispensation of grace. This fountain is open to the
"house of David and inhabitants of Jerusalem," at
which time a nation shall be born in a day. As
Joseph comforted his brethren so Christ will comfort His brethren, the Jews. Stephen in his apology
takes up this train of thought and says, "And at the
second time Joseph was made known to his brethren."
(Acts 7:13). Likewise, at the **second time** or the
second appearance of Christ, He will be made known
unto His brethren, the Jews. They rejected Him at
His first coming and took part in His crucifixion, pictured by the selling of Joseph into Egypt, for they
wanted to do away with Him. However, at His second
appearance to His brethren, they will acknowledge
their sin for which they will be forgiven, and then
they will enter into the thousand years of millennial reign. As Naomi took the child and laid it on
her bosom, expressing her affection and devotion, so
the Jewish remnant nation will embrace Jesus, the
Savior of the world, with love and affection when the
veil has been removed from their eyes. How it thrills
our hearts as we think of the love of God in working
out the great plan of redemption in bringing lost men
to Himself. This brings us to the last division of this
study.

C. THE BIRTH AND THE MANGER. (v's. 18-
22). Under this division we note the term *"the generations of."* This phrase is found eleven times in
the Book of Genesis. It occurs first in chapter 2:4,

"the generations of the heavens and of the earth."
The first four chapters form the introduction of the
Book of Genesis. The remainder of the Book is
divided into ten divisions by the words *"the generations of,"* which are as follows:

Gen. 5:1 to 6:8.
    "The Generations of Adam."
Gen. 6:9 to 9:29.
    "The Generations of Noah."
Gen. 10:1 to 11:9.
    "The Generations of the Sons of Noah."
Gen. 11:10 to 11:26.
    "The Generations of Shem."
Gen. 11:27 to 25:11.
    "The Generations of Terah."
Gen. 25:12 to 25:18.
    "The Generations of Ishmael."
Gen. 25:19 to 35:29.
    "The Generations of Isaac."
Gen. 36:1 to 36:8.
    "The Generations of Esau." (In Canaan)
Gen. 36:9 to 37:1.
    "The Generations of Esau."   (In Mount Seir)
Gen. 37:2 to 50:26.
    "The Generations of Jacob."

If the reader will look up these references, he will
note that the generations of Ishmael and Esau, which
represent men after the flesh, are summarized in fifty
verses while the men who are included in the genealogy of Jesus Christ cover nearly all of the Book. The
identity with Christ made the difference. The ten
generations forming the ten divisions of the Book of
Genesis show man's obligation to God as ten is the

number of responsibility. The following are three
other references to this term in the Old Testament:
Exodus 6:16-19.
"The Sons of Levi according to their Generations."
Numbers 3:1.
"The Generations of Aaron and Moses."
Ruth 4:18.
"The Generations of Pharez."

This makes a total of fourteen generations found
in the Old Testament, signifying a double perfection.
The generations of Pharez, which we are now considering in the closing verses of the Book of Ruth, includes ten names, concluding with David, the son of
Jesse, who is the central figure in the Old Testament.
It was to him that the Lord *"swore"* in truth—*"Of the
fruit of thy body will I set upon thy throne."* (Psalm
132:11). This same truth was uttered by the prophet
Jeremiah: *"Behold, the days come, saith the Lord,
that I will raise unto David a righteous Branch, and
a King shall reign and prosper, and shall execute
judgment and justice in the earth."* (Jer. 23:5). The
people in Christ's time who understood the Scriptures reminded Christ of the same truth when they
said, *"Hath not the scripture said, That Christ cometh
of the seed of David?"* (John 7:42). Paul in writing
to the Church of Rome told them that Jesus Christ
*"was made of the seed of David according to the
flesh,"* (Rom. 1:3); that is, the genealogy of Jesus
Christ can be traced back to the house of David.
(Matt. 1:6). God had promised that He would *"raise
unto David a righteous Branch."* (Jer. 23:5). Jesus
acknowledged this seedline when He declared Himself to be *"the root and the offspring of David."* (Rev.

22:16). David is the root out of which the *"Branch"* (Christ) sprang. Thus, we see that the generations of the Old Testament climax with the name David, from whom came Jesus Christ, the Savior of the world. This seed of David is not only called a *"Branch,"* but also a *"King."* (Jer. 23:5). This office of King, Christ has never held. He was a prophet in the days of His flesh while here on earth; He is now engaged in the high priestly functions on the right hand of God. The office of King, He is yet going to hold in order that the promises given to David may be fulfilled. This truth was foretold by Ezekiel, (chapter 37), where he pictures the regathering of Judah and Israel to their own land, (v. 21), the land of Palestine. He further states that *"David my servant shall be king over them."* (v. 24). This can be no other than Christ, Who takes on the name of David, for the same promise was given to Mary, (Luke 1:31-33), when the angels said, *"The Lord God shall give unto him (Jesus) the throne of his father David: And he shall reign over the house of Jacob for ever; and of his kingdom there shall be no end."* The reader should notice the seven promises, with seven *"shalts"* and *"shalls"* in these three verses. Four of these have been fulfilled, and the other three are yet to be fulfilled.

In the genealogy of Jesus Christ as recorded by Matthew, chapter one, there are four women mentioned of whom two were strangers to the commonwealth of Israel. These were Rachab (Rahab), a Canaanite, and Ruth, of the country of Moab; both of these were Gentiles. From this we see that the

Gentile strangers and foreigners are welcomed into
the body of Christ, into the citizenship of the saints.
The other two women were Thamar and Bathsheba,
the wife of Urias. Thus, we find that the last word
of the Book of Ruth is **"David"** from whom came
Jesus Christ, the Savior of the world.

RUTH ON THE ROAD OF REDEMPTION
STUDY EIGHT

In this study we shall consider Ruth as a type of a sinner in his progress from sin to salvation. Every sinner who is redeemed and eventually united in marriage to Jesus Christ will, in a measure, follow her footsteps. Note the following seven steps—

AS A SINNER SHE FREQUENTED HIS HOUSE.

AS A STRANGER SHE FOUND HIS GRACE.

AS A DAUGHTER SHE FELT HIS LOVE.

AS A GLEANER SHE FOLLOWED HIS WORD.

AS A WORSHIPER SHE FELL AT HIS FEET.

AS A HANDMAIDEN SHE FED AT HIS TABLE.

AS A BRIDE SHE FINISHED HIS PLAN.

I. AS A SINNER SHE FREQUENTED HIS HOUSE.

As Ruth came to the house of Boaz, chapter 2:7, and there communed with the reapers and the servant of Boaz, a type of the Holy Spirit, so a sinner should attend the house of God that he might hear the Word preached. It was there Ruth became acquainted with Boaz and received instructions from him. There are very few people who are saved in their homes or in other places outside of the church. That is where the Gospel is preached, where, as a rule, a sinner can find God. If a person with an honest heart will frequently attend the services in the house of God, he will soon find the way of salvation. Special efforts in the nature of revival meetings and

Bible conferences are often held in the house of God for the purpose of attracting the sinner to the place of worship where he can hear the truth, which, if accepted will make him free. The trouble with many people is that they attend one service and are so gripped with conviction that they refuse to come again, continuing carelessly in the old life of sin. Reader, if you are unsaved, frequently attend the house of God and learn for yourself the truth of salvation.

II.   AS A STRANGER SHE FOUND HIS GRACE.

It was not long after Ruth had visited the house of Boaz that she became a partaker of his grace and asked in astonishment, *"Why have I found grace in thine eyes?"* (Chap. 2:10). There are three items relative to grace in the Word of God, namely, the God of grace, the throne of grace, and the Spirit of grace. (1) **It originated by the God of grace.** (I Pet. 5:10). Here God is called *"the God of all grace,"* showing it originated by Him. (2) **It is obtained from the throne of grace.** A new and living way has been opened whereby man can approach God at the throne of grace. Grace is not obtained from deacons, elders, preachers, or priests but directly from God, Himself. We are urged to come boldly to this *"throne of grace."* (Heb. 4:16). (3) **It is offered by the Spirit of grace.** In Hebrews 10:29 the Holy Spirit is called the Spirit of grace. That name is given to Him because when He comes to the sinner He offers to impart the wonderful grace of God into his heart and life that he might enjoy the benefits of the atonement.

The Trinity can be seen in these three items. The

Holy Spirit (Spirit of Grace) first comes to the sinner introducing to him the Gospel of grace. Jesus, the second person of the Trinity, Who is now occupying the *"Throne of Grace,"* invites men to come boldly on the basis of atonement that He might plead their case. When the sinner has accepted this invitation, he has access by Him unto the Father. (Eph. 2:18). From this we see that the Trinity is involved in redemption for man. (Heb. 9:14). When Ruth found his grace it portrayed the sinner finding the *"grace of God"* manifested in His Son Jesus and brought to man by the Holy Ghost.

III.   AS A DAUGHTER SHE FELT HIS LOVE.

When Ruth said, *"Thou hast comforted me,"* (chap. 2:13), it was equivalent to saying, *"I have felt your love,"* for love brings comfort. Just what the love of Boaz was to Ruth, the love of Christ is to us. The term the *"love of Christ"* is found three times in the Bible. (1) **It is inconceivable in its estimation.** "And to know the love of Christ, which passeth knowledge." (Eph. 3:19). No man is able to conceive with his mental capacity the wonderful love of Christ, for it passes all knowledge. Men are able to estimate some things and to reason out other things, but the love of Christ, according to Paul's statement here, passes all knowledge and reason. It is beyond anything that man can comprehend. Jesus said, *"As the Father hath loved me, so have I loved you."* If you can imagine how God loved His only Son Christ, then you may know how Christ loves you. (2) **It is imperative in its operation.** *"For the love of Christ constraineth us."* (II Cor. 5: 14). It was the love of Christ in Paul's life that caused him to so live that men thought he was beside himself or, in terms of today, insane. He was so endowed with the love of Christ that he worked, toiled, and labored unceasingly night and day for lost men. The love of Christ surely is imperative (obligatory) in its operation. It was this love that forced Moffat to Africa, Hudson to India, and Taylor to China. (3) **It is inseparable in its manifestation.** *"Who shall separate us from the love of Christ? shall tribulation, or distress, or persecution, or famine, or nakedness, or peril, or sword?"* (Rom. 8:35). The love of Christ is so great that it will cause men to endure tribulation or distress. It will take one through starvation and nakedness, through perils of all descriptions, (II Cor. 11:26), and, if necessary, through martyrdom by the sword. The love of Christ is so binding and uniting to His cause that untold numbers have laid down their lives in martyrdom for it.

Many people wonder what it is that makes tender the stern man's spirit, that revives the cruel man's love, that removes the grouchy man's hatred, that opens the stingy man's purse, that alters the worldly man's plan, that changes the selfish man's vision, and softens the rebellious man's heart. It is nothing but the *"love of Christ."* As Ruth felt the love of Boaz, the sinner actually feels the *"love of Christ."*

IV. AS A GLEANER SHE FOLLOWED HIS WORD.

If we expect to continue in His fellowship and retain our relationship, we must be gleaners in His Word as Ruth was in the field of Boaz. Christian growth is impossible without the study of the Word. The Word of God has a great part in the Christian's life. Note the sevenfold admonition—We should hearken to it **reverently,** for it is God's voice to us on the printed page. We should study it **prayerfully,** for it will reveal our ruin, redemption, and restoration. We should follow it **obediently,** for it will condemn or acquit us at the judgment bar of God. We should practice it **earnestly,** for it is the true source of all pleasure and happiness in this life. We should trust it **completely,** for the precepts and promises never fail. We should proclaim it **faithfully,** for it is God's final revelation and warning to lost men. We should search it **diligently,** for it contains practical, devotional, and inspirational truth for the child of God. If we do this, our life will be wholesome, our love will be active, and our labour for Him will be a pleasure.

The preciousness and sweetness of the Word of God is portrayed in the experience that came to Ezekiel, (chap. 3:1-3), when he was handed a roll (scroll) and was commanded to eat the contents of the roll. After he had obeyed the commands of the Lord, Ezekiel says, "*It was in my mouth as honey for sweetness.*" In like manner, the Word of God today has a sweet taste to the Christian. The seven following phrases are words of sweetness to the weary gleaner: (1) **Words of Affection.** (John 15:9). Christ is comparing the love that God had for Him with the love that He had for His disciples and states, "*As the Father hath loved me, so have I loved you.*" As the gleaner studies the Word, he will see the greatness of the love of God for him. (2) **Words of Forgiveness.**

(Luke 7:48). To the weeping woman who washed His feet with her tears and wiped them with the hairs of her head, Jesus said, *"Thy sins are forgiven."* God not only gives man the assurance of his forgiveness through the inner consciousness of his being but also through the written pages of His Word. (3) **Words of Cheer.** (John 16:33). The last words of the discourses of Jesus to His disciples before the crucifixion were: *"In the world ye shall have tribulation: but be of good cheer; I have overcome the world."* The world, which is evil in its nature, contaminating in its influence, antagonistic in its spirit, and downward in its tendency, is the place through which we must pass. In the world Christ was crucified; against its evil we must testify; and by it we are hated. To the storm-tossed, persecuted pilgrim He speaks from His Word today and says, *"Be of good cheer; I have overcome the world.* (4) **Words of Grace.** (John 8:11). The Pharisees brought to Jesus the woman who had been caught in the act of immorality. They stated that Moses in his law commanded that such should be stoned but requested that Christ give His opinion concerning the matter. After Jesus had revealed the Pharisees' sins by writing on the ground, they departed in haste, leaving the woman alone with Jesus. Her accusers had fled, and now there was no one to condemn her. Then Jesus spoke unto her saying, *"Neither do I condemn thee: go, and sin no more."* The lesson is one of law and grace. Law that demanded death and stoning, in type, had passed away when the Pharisees were no longer there to condemn her, and grace reigned in its place when Jesus said, *"Neither do I condemn thee."* So the gleaner in the

Word will find that the law no longer condemns him who has heard these sweet words of grace, *"Neither do I condemn thee."*   (5) **Words of Comfort.** (John 14:1-3). In these verses we find that Christ speaks of His Father's house of many mansions and that He is going to prepare a place for those who believe in Him, but there is still a greater comfort than the preparing of the place, and that is that He will come again to receive us unto Himself that we may be with Him in His Father's house. These verses should be the cure for all heart trouble. What a comfort it is to the weary pilgrim to know that this wicked world with all of its sorrow, cares, and strife is not our eternal abiding place, but we, like Abraham, look for a city whose Builder and Maker is God. From that thought we receive our comfort. (6) **Words of Hope.** *"Behold, I come quickly."* (Rev. 22:7). The hope of the Church through all ages has been the second Coming of Christ. For that reason Peter called it a **"living hope"** because it continued to live from one generation to another. Paul called it a **"blessed hope,"** meaning a happy hope—a hope that fills the heart with joy and anticipation. John called it a **purifying hope,** for everyone that has the hope of Christ, the second return, purifies himself by walking in the light of full salvation and practical holiness. (7) **Words of Victory.** (Rev. 1:18). In this chapter He Who was crucified exclaims, *"I am alive forevermore, Amen; and have the keys of hell and of death."* Here we have a Christ, victorious over death, hell, and the grave. If the reader will glean in the Word, he will find sweet words of affection, forgiveness, cheer, grace, comfort, hope, and victory as we have just reviewed.

V.   AS A WORSHIPER SHE FELL AT HIS FEET.

As Ruth fell at the feet of Boaz so others came to the feet of Jesus. (1) Mary Magdalene **stood** at His feet weeping. (Luke 7:38). She, (like Ruth), was a Gentile, as can be seen by the words of Simon: *"This man, if he were a prophet, would have known who and what manner of woman this is."* In the word *"who,"* it gives her nationality. She was an outcast, a Gentile. *"What manner"* describes her character, for she was a sinner. However, she left His feet justified in the eyes of the on-lookers and justified with God. (2) The demoniac **sat** at His feet. (Luke 8:35). Another Gentile, who had been delivered from the power of Satan, now was sitting, clothed and in his right mind, at the feet of the Master of all circumstances. (3) The Syrophenician woman, (a Gentile), **worshiped** at His feet, (Mark 7:25). There she received mercy as she had requested, and her daughter was gloriously healed. As this Syrophenician woman worshiped at the feet of Christ so we can do likewise in this age and acknowledge that He is all and in all. These three Gentiles presented themselves at the feet of Jesus as Ruth, the Gentile, did at the feet of Boaz. Here we see the forecast and typical teaching concerning the Gentiles in the little Book of Ruth.

VI.   AS A HANDMAIDEN SHE FED AT HIS TABLE.

The fact that she fed at his table gives the thought

of fellowship and communion, for the table of shew-bread in the Tabernacle was typical of the same, while the golden altar represented intercession and the candlestick was figurative of testimony. As Mephibosheth sat at David's table, (II Sam. 9:13), Pharoah's daughter sat at Solomon's table, (Song of Sol. 1:12, 2:3-4), and Ruth sat at the table of Boaz, so we can, in the same manner, enjoy fellowship and communion with Jesus Christ around the Lord's table. These Old Testament lessons not only point forward to this dispensation in which we are now living, but also to the time when another table shall be made ready. Christ spoke of this when He said, *"And I appoint unto you a kingdom, as my Father hath appointed unto me; That ye may eat and drink at my table in my kingdom."* (Luke 22:29, 30). There we shall sit down with Abraham, Isaac, and Jacob and enjoy constant and eternal fellowship.

VII. AS A BRIDE SHE FINISHED HIS PLAN.

In a previous study I told how Boaz hinted to Ruth of his plan of marrying her. He did this by urging her to remain with his maidens until the end of the harvest. (Chap. 2:21). At last *"she finished his plan"* by uniting with him in marriage. When the bride of Christ finishes His plan (which was started before the foundations of the world, (Eph. 1:4), He shall see the travail of His soul and be satisfied, as was predicted by Isaiah. (Chap. 53:10, 11). Then His comfort and satisfaction will be complete. There will be seven things with which He shall be satisfied:

1. He shall be satisfied with the accomplishments

of His death. After the fall of Adam and Eve, three curses were pronounced. **First,** the punishment meted to the woman was a multiplication of sorrow. (Gen. 3:16). Jesus, in the Messianic prophecy of Isaiah, is called the Man of Sorrows. (Chap. 53:3). In the Garden of Gethsemane He said, *"My soul is exceeding sorrowful, even until death."* From this we see that on the cross He bore the sorrows of mankind. **Second,** to Adam it was said, *"In the sweat of thy face shalt thou eat bread."* (Gen. 3:19). This curse has been resting on mankind ever since that time, and truly it has been fulfilled. In the hours of the atonement, Christ sweat great drops of blood that in the coming age this curse, *("In the sweat of thy face shalt thou eat bread"),* might be lifted from mankind. **Third,** the ground too was cursed for man's sin—*"Thorns also and thistles shall it bring forth."* (Gen. 3:18). However, the day is coming when, instead of thorns and briars, the fir and the myrtle trees will be growing in abundance. (Isaiah 55:13). The warning to Adam was *"in the day that thou eatest thereof (the forbidden fruit) thou shalt surely die."* (Gen. 2:17). The prediction has come true, and in every class, climate, and country we find death striking its fatal blow, but Jesus entered death's domain, tasted its sting, endured its agony and conquered its destiny that we might be free from its claims. He shall be satisfied to know that the punishment and penalty of sin has been fully met by Himself.

2. **He shall be satisfied with the Church which He has redeemed.** This Church, His body, will come forth without *"spot, or wrinkle . . . holy and without blem-*

ish." Here we have the character of this body whom He has redeemed—a holy people for a holy Heaven. A sanctifying and cleansing work of redemption has been accomplished in their lives *"that he might present it (the church) to himself."* When He has received the Church unto Himself, He shall be satisfied with it.

3. **He shall be satisfied with His work of intercession.** For nearly two thousand years He has been engaged in the work of intercession for the salvation of lost men and the cleansing and keeping of the believer. The answer to His prayer is seen in the innumerable multitude found in Revelation 5:11. This multitude will consist *"of every kindred, and tongue, and people, and nation."* This shows that His life of intercession has gone to the uttermost parts of the earth. Men in all states and conditions, some in the lowest depths of degradation, are included in this multitude. When He sees the accomplishment of His intercession, He shall be satisfied.

4. **He shall be satisfied with His thousand years of reign,** which He is to have on earth. This reign will be one of righteousness. *"Behold, a king shall reign in righteousness, and princes shall rule in judgment."* (Isaiah 32:1). It will be a perfect reign with no political corruptness, dishonest financiers, and immoral society; righteousness shall go from shore to shore. It is at this time that God shall give Him the heathen for His inheritance and the uttermost parts of the earth as His possession. He shall then rule with a rod of iron, and the disobedient shall be broken as a potter's vessel. (Psalm 2:8, 9). No doubt the conversion

of the heathen will be a great comfort to His heart; it will be His satisfaction.

5. **He shall be satisfied with the restoration of the Heavens and the earth.** The heavens and earth will be renovated and restored to their original order. Every particle of sin, in act or principle, will be completely destroyed with no possibility of it ever re-entering the universe. This means that atonement will never again be necessary. His triumph over sin will thus be determined. There will be no heaven with a darkening cloud nor atmosphere that breeds tornadoes. The earth will never again be rocked by a quake, covered by darkness, flooded by water, nor purged by fire. When this is restored, it will be His satisfaction.

6. **He shall be satisfied with the punishment of Satan and the wicked.** Satan, the Antichrist, and the false prophet will be cast into the lake of fire. He who polluted the universe, deceived the nations, wrecked homes, and robbed many of their Heavenly hope will be sentenced to his eternal doom to the satisfaction of Christ. The records of the wicked will reveal that great opportunity has been offered them to be saved. The love of God, the blood of Christ, the conviction of the Spirit, the preaching of the Gospel and the services of the Church will be the evidence that no stone was left unturned that men might be redeemed. It will be revealed that man's destiny was settled by his own choice and that by his own volition he sought his own place. As a man who refuses to escape from a burning building, that he might reclaim some of his hoarded treasures to be spent upon

himself, must perish in the flames, so those who reject Christ must suffer eternal punishment. Christ will rest assured that everything possible has been done to redeem those who will have their portion in the lake of fire. This will be His satisfaction.

7. **He shall be satisfied with His bride, of which Ruth is a type.** Just as Ruth finished the plan of Boaz so the bride of Christ will complete the plan of the ages when she becomes His wife. It will comfort and satisfy the heart of Christ to know that this blood-bought bride is His eternally. He shall find His delight in her whom He so dearly loves. As Abraham sent Eliezer to get a bride for Isaac so the Spirit of God is calling men to repentance and salvation that eventually the plan of God may be completed, in having a bride for His Son Jesus, as portrayed in the romance of Ruth and Boaz. The Scriptures state that Rebecca, the wife of Isaac, comforted him after the death of his mother, Sarah. (Gen. 24:67). It will be remembered that Jesus wept over Jerusalem, the mother of Israel, but after His death and resurrection He was comforted by the thought of having a new bride, who, in a measure, was to take the place of Israel. Thus we see that Christ will have a sevenfold satisfaction in His eternal home.

BOAZ THE BUYER AND BRIDEGROOM

STUDY NINE

Ruth's Romance of Redemption would not be complete if we did not write a final chapter on Boaz as a type of Christ. As the reader sees Christ in the life of Boaz, may it strengthen his ambitions, enlarge his inspirations, centralize his attentions, increase his devotions, and quicken his aspirations. Note the sevenfold type—

I. THE REDEEMER KINSMAN.

The word *"kinsman"* means *"a relative."* In order that Boaz might be a redeemer, it was necessary that he be a relative of Ruth. In like manner, it was necessary that Jesus be born of a woman to take upon Himself the seed of Abraham, which gives us the mystery of the incarnation. We can now say with Naomi, *"The man is near of kin unto us, one of our next kinsmen."* (Chap. 2:20). The word *"kinsman"* is found fourteen times in the Book. $(2 \times 7 = 14$. A double perfection). In several places in the margin it reads: *"One that hath the right to redeem."* The Hebrew word *"goel,"* which is translated *"kinsman"* in Ruth 3:13, is translated *"ransom"* in Isaiah 51:10 and *"redeemer"* in Job 19:25, where Job says, "I know that my redeemer (goel) liveth."

In order for Jesus Christ to become our Redeemer, three things were necessary: (1) He **"was made flesh."** (John 1:14). The flesh speaks of the mortality of man. (Psalm 78:39). This enabled Christ, the Holy Son of God, to die; He was *"put to death in the flesh."* (I

Pet. 3:18). (2) He **"hath made him to be sin for us."**
(II Cor. 5:21). As the sins of Israel were laid upon the
head of the scapegoat, which bore their iniquity, so
our sins were laid on Him as Isaiah declared: *"The
Lord hath laid on him the iniquity of us all."* (Chap.
53:6). This load of sin was so heavy that it crushed
Him to the ground in the Garden of Gethsemane. The
effect of the great weight of sin may be observed by
the fact that He sweat great drops of blood. (3) He
was **"made like unto his brethren."** (Heb. 2:17). The
purpose of this was that He might be tempted in all
points, as we are, that He might be a faithful High
Priest and be able to succor those who are tempted.
Thus, He was made flesh, **His incarnation;** He was
made sin, **His crucifixion;** He was made like unto
His brethren, **His intercession** as High Priest on the
right hand of God.

II. THE BUYER AT THE GATE.

In this verse, chapter 4:4, we find the words *"redeem it"* five times. The thought of the chapter is
redemption. You will note—(1) **A Personal Redemption.** Boaz, himself, had to buy it personally, and he
had to redeem Ruth, herself, personally. From this
we observe that redemption is individual. The clarion
note of the Gospel is: *"Whosoever will, may come."*
(2) **A Public Redemption.** It was not done in the
dark or behind closed doors but at the gate of the city
in the presence of the elders. In the same manner, as
Moses smote the rock in the presence of the elders,
(Ex. 17:5), so Christ was smitten in the presence of
the elders of His time. (Matt. 27:41). (3) **A Powerful Redemption.** It was powerful enough to remove

the near kinsman, the old man, and to buy back the lost property, which was in the hands of him who held the mortgage. Today the redemption of Jesus Christ is powerful enough to meet the needs of every sinner regardless of his condition. (4) **A Productive Redemption.** "And she bare a son." (Chap. 4:13). A profession of salvation which does not reproduce the life of Christ is not the salvation that Jesus offers. He saves us that we might bear fruit. A Christian is likened to *"a tree planted by the rivers of water, that bringeth forth his fruit in his season; his leaf also shall not wither; and whatsoever he doeth shall prosper."* (Psalm 1:3). Notice four things concerning the Christian in this verse. He is—

1. **Planted.**

   "By the rivers of water."

2. **Productive.**

   "Bringeth forth his fruit in his season."

3. **Perpetual.**

   "His leaf also shall not wither."

4. **Prosperous.**

   "Whatsoever he doeth shall prosper."

(5)   **A Pleasing Redemption.** (Chap. 4:11, 12). Just as this redemption pleased the women of Ruth's day so redemption is pleasing today. It pleases the heart of God, and the angels of God, the Church of God, and the redeemed of God. Eternity alone will tell how many homes have been made happy because of this redemption.   (6) **A Perfect Redemption.** *"So Boaz took Ruth, and she was his wife."* (Chap. 4:13). The redemption of Boaz set aside every hindering cause and reclaimed all that was lost, even the name of the

dead. In like manner the redemption of Jesus Christ
is so perfect and complete that all that was lost in the
fall of man shall be regained, and after the Marriage
of the Lamb has taken place, the millennium has run
its course, and the Ages of Ages has set in, there will
be no possibility of the world being ruined by another
fall. (7) **A Prophetic Redemption.** The redemption
of Boaz was a type and figure of a great redemption,
which was to take place. This, the redemption of Jesus Christ, we are enjoying today. The plan of God
has been that He might obtain a bride for His Son
Jesus just as Boaz obtained Ruth for his own. By the
many signs around us, it appears that the marriage
of this bride to Christ is not far distant.

III. THE RESTORER OF LIFE.

"He shall be unto thee a restorer of thy life." (Ruth
4:15). Christianity can be summed up in one word,
and that is *"life,"* new life in Christ Jesus whereby
old things pass away and all things become new. Jesus said, *"I am come that they might have life, and
that they might have it more abundantly."* (John 10:
10). The reader will note it speaks of both *"life"* and
"the more abundant life," which refers respectively
to the birth of the Spirit and the baptism of the Spirit.
The trouble with many professors of religion today is
that they have never been born again. There is no
Divine life functioning in their lives; real life is always manifested. There's also dispensational teaching in the above verse, for as Boaz was to be a restorer of life to Naomi so Jesus is to be a restorer of
life to the Jewish nation in the last days when the
fig tree shall bud, blossom, and bear fruit (take on

life). They will then return to their own land, Palestine, followed by a thousand years of peace on
earth.

IV.   THE PROVIDER OF GRACE.

The word *"grace"* is found three times in the second
chapter. (1) **The minister of grace.** "In whose sight I
shall find grace." (v. 2). Just as Boaz was a minister
or giver of grace so Christ is the One Who bestows
this unmerited favor upon us. The closing verse of the
Bible contains the benediction—*"The grace of our
Lord Jesus Christ be with you all. Amen."* (Rev. 22:
21). His grace has been with us thus far throughout
this dispensation and shall continue until its close. (2)
The marvel of grace. "Why have I found grace in
thine eyes?" (v. 10). She marvels why she, a Moabitish damsel, should have his unmerited favor. Many
a child of God has felt the same way when he sees
scores, with whom he has formerly associated, still
without God while he is enjoying the rich blessings
that grace bestows. (3) **The merit of grace.** "I find
favour in thy sight." (Chap. 2:13, margin). The word
"favour" means *"grace"* according to the Hebrew.
She acknowledged that it was through his grace she
had been comforted even though she, unlike his own
handmaidens, was a stranger in Israel. She, in this
verse, is showing her appreciation for what Boaz has
done. We have received, in like manner, the comfort that grace bestows.

V.   THE GIVER OF REST.

Boaz is a type of Christ in relation to rest. As he
provided rest for Ruth so Christ provides soul rest for

the Gentiles of this age. There are four things required to obtain constant and perfect soul-rest: (1) A
revelation of our own hearts by the Word of God.   If
we do not see ourselves in the light of God's Word,
we will remain in darkness.   (2) An emancipation
from the life of sin by the power of God.   He is the
only One Who can raise us from the mighty grip and
power of sin.   (3) A sanctified life for service in the
Kingdom of God.   God does not want lazy Christians;
they were not found in Gideon's three hundred or in
the one hundred and twenty tarrying in the upper
room. God's purpose in saving us is that we should be
of service to Him and others.   (4) A testimony of the
mighty grace of God.   A man will soon lose his communion with God by failing to testify of what God
has done for him, thus forfeiting his soul-rest.   The
first letter of these four words—Revelation, Emancipation, Sanctified, and Testimony—make an acrostic
for the word "rest."

A   Revelation from the Word of God.
An   Emancipation through the power of God.
A   Sanctified life by the Spirit of God.
A   Testimony to the grace of God.

VI. THE REWARDER OF SERVICE.

*"Every man shall receive his own reward according
to his own labour."* (I Cor. 3:8). In this chapter three
things are mentioned concerning the service and the
work man does. (1) **"Every man's work shall be made
manifest."** (v. 13). This shows a record is being kept
of what we do.   Whether we are the laymen in the
pew, the pastor in the pulpit, or a higher official in the
church, a record is being kept of our services in the

Kingdom. (2) **Every man's work shall be tried.** "Fire shall try every man's work." (v. 13). The motive back of our labor will be the test. If what we have done has been done in His name and for His glory we shall receive our reward. We are not rewarded because we are Christians, for we are saved by free grace, but the reward comes as a result of the good works we have done in His Name. In Mark 9:41 Jesus states that "Whosoever shall give you a cup of water to drink in my name, because you belong to Christ, he shall not lose his reward." (3) **Every man's work shall be rewarded.** (v. 14). Some works shall be destroyed by fire with no reward for the labor bestowed. Many have worked in the name of their churches or that they might receive the applause of man. Others for a financial gain, not for the glory of God, have preached the Gospel, written books, or performed some other sort of labor. Many hard tasks will be burned because the motive behind them was personal or ecclesiastical. Others will be rewarded in the eternal home for the works performed here because what they did was exclusively for the glory of God. Paul mentions that the foundation, which is Jesus Christ, has already been tried and has stood the test. Likewise, all who build upon it must be tried. May the reader and the writer be so aided by the Spirit that what we do in word, thought, or deed may be for the exaltation of Jesus Christ and for the glory of God.

VII. THE LOVER IN MARRIAGE.

"Ye are witnesses this day that . . . Ruth the Moabitess, the wife of Mahlon, have I purchased to be my

wife." (Chap. 4:9, 10). He did not buy her to be a housekeeper or to be a slave, but to be his wife, one whom he could love and cherish, one with whom he could have fellowship. Fellowship and communion have resulted in union. It points forward to the day when the Church of Jesus Christ shall sit down with Him at the Marriage of the Lamb. Boaz, the richest man in Bethlehem-judah, took a stranger and an outcast and says, *"I have purchased (her) to be my wife."* Ruth had received permission to glean in the fields of Boaz and had received handfuls on purpose and six measures of barley. Now she receives something even greater than a field of grain or a mansion on his estate; she receives Boaz, himself, as her lover in marriage. Likewise, Jesus said, *"I will come again, and receive you unto myself; that where I am, there ye may be also."* (John 14:3). What a great event that will be; every trial, misunderstanding, heartache, temptation, failure, and sorrow will be gone forever. There we will be in the presence of righteousness, holiness, peace, and joy forevermore. The Bride of Jesus Christ will never be satisfied until united in marriage with Him, our Heavenly Boaz.

Well might Naomi now ask Ruth, *"Who art thou?"* as she did in chapter 3:16. Ruth could now make the happy reply, *"I am the wife of Boaz."* In like manner, if the world and those mocking and scoffing rejecters could ask the bride at the Marriage of the Lamb, *"Who art thou?"* she could reply in grace, splendor, and exaltation, *"I am the bride of Christ."* No longer will we be, like Ruth, strangers and outcasts of Israel, but through the countless ages of eternity we shall be the happy companions of Jesus Christ. This marriage will be followed with a honeymoon of a thousand years, the millennial age, which will be short compared to eternity. This marriage will never be annulled by death or court or marred by strife, misunderstanding, or sin. Such are the prospects that are just ahead for those who will follow Ruth in surrender, separation, and service. The culmination of their Christian life will be no other than a marriage to Jesus Christ and a home in the place which is now being prepared for those who love Him.

THE END